D0613767

The LITTLE BLACK SONGBOOK
SONGBOOK

Amsco Publications
A part of **The Music Sales Group**
New York/London/Paris/Sydney/Copenhagen/Berlin/Tokyo/Madrid

Order No. AM986029
ISBN-10: 0-8256-3574-8
ISBN-13: 978-0-8256-3574-8

Layout: Sol y Luna Creations

Exclusive Distributors:
Music Sales Corporation
257 Park Avenue South, New York, NY, 10010 USA
Music Sales Limited
14/15 Berners Street, London W1T 3LJ, England
Music Sales Pty. Limited
120 Rothschild Street, Rosebery, Sydney, NSW 2018, Australia

Printed in Peru by Quebecor World

www.musicsales.com

Ain't No Fun (Waiting 'Round To Be A Millionaire)

Words & Music by
Angus Young, Malcolm Young and Bon Scott

Intro

‖: **D5** | | |

| **G5 G5/A G5/B** | **Csus2 G5/B G5** :‖

‖: **D5**   **D6** | **D5**   **D6** :‖ *play 7 times*

Verse 1

D5   **D6**   **D5 D6**   **D5** *cont. sim.*
Well I left my job in my hometown,

And I headed for the smoke.

Got a rock 'n' roll band and a fast right hand,

Gonna get to the top.

Nothing's gonna stop us, no, nothin'.

So if you've got the money, we've got the sound.

You put it up, and we'll put it down.

If you got the dollar, we got the song.

Just wanna boogie woogie all night long.

Yeah, boogie.

Verse 2

D5   **D6 D5**   **D6 D5**   *cont. sim.*

I got holes in my shoes, I got holes in my teeth,

I got holes in my socks, I can't get no sleep.

I'm tryin' to make a million.

An' I got patches, on the patches,

On my old blue jeans.

Well, they used to be blue, when they used to be new,

When they used to be clean.

But I've got a mama who's a hummer,

Just keepin' me alive.

While I'm in the band room drinkin' with the boys,

She's workin' nine to five.

But just you wait.

One of these days see me drivin' 'round town,

In my rock 'n' Rolls Royce (with) the sun roof down.

My bottle of booze,

No summertime blues,

Shouting loud, "Look at me,"

In my rock 'n' roll voice.

Chorus 1

        G5   **G5/A**
‖: No it ain't no fun,
G5/B **Csus2**   **D5**
Waitin' 'round to be a millionaire.   :‖
        G5   **G5/A**
‖: No it ain't no fun,
G5/B **Csus2**   **D5**
Waitin' 'round to be a millionaire.   :‖

Interlude

‖: **D5** | | :‖
‖: **D5** **D6 D5 D6 D5** | **D6** **D5 D6 D5** :‖ *play 5 times*

Chorus 2

       D5
‖: Well, it ain't no fun, oh no.

No, it ain't no fun. That's what I said! :‖

Waitin' 'round to be a millionaire.

‖: Ain't no fun,

Waitin' 'round to be a millionaire. :‖ *repeat ad lib. to fade*

Are You Ready

Words & Music by
Angus Young and Malcolm Young

Intro

‖: **Dsus2** | **Cadd9** | **G6/B** |
| **Cadd9** :‖ **Dsus2** | **Dadd9/F♯** |
| **G6** | **Dm9/F** | | |
‖: **D5 C5 D5** | **F5 C5 G5**:‖ *play 3 times*
| **D5 C5 D5** |

Verse 1

F5   C5 G5 D5 C5
Sweet   apple pie,
D5   F5   C5
   Standing in the street,
     G5 D5 C5
Hands outta line,
D5   F5   C5
   Looking for some meat.
     G5   D5 C5
She'll take you high,
D5   F5 C5
When you feel her sting.
    G5   D5 C5
She'll make you fly,
D5   F5   C5 G5
Then you know you're coming.

Chorus 1

Dsus2   Dadd9/F♯
Who all need it, who?
G6/9   Fmaj13
Who all need it, you!
Dsus2   Dadd9/F♯
Who all need it, who all need it? Yes you do!
G6/9   F6
You all breathe it, we all need it.
    D5   C5 D5   C5 G/B
‖: Are you ready for a good   time?
C5   G/B   D/A   G/B   C5 G/B
   Then get ready for the night   line.   :‖
N.C.   F5
Are you ready for a good time?

Verse 2

| C5 | G5 | D5 C5 D5 | F5 | C5 |

She's making eyes,   at everything she meet.

| | G5 D5 | C5 D5 | F5 | C5 |

Ain't it a crime,   when she make you pump heat.

| | G5 | D5 C5 D5 | F5 C5 |

She'll make you fly,   because that's her thing.

| | G5 | D5 C5 |

She make you dry,

| D5 | | F5 | C5 | G5 |

Then you know you're   bro - - ken in.

Chorus 2

Dsus2   **Dadd9/F♯**

Who all need it, who?

G6/9   **Fmaj13**

Who all need it, you!

Dsus2   **Dadd9/F♯**

Who all need it, who all need it? Yes you do.

G6/9   **F6**

You all breathe it, we all need it.

| | D5 | C5 | D5 | C5 | G/B |

‖: Are you ready for a good   time?

| C5 | G/B | D/A | G/B | C5 | G/B |

   Then get ready for the night   line.   :‖

N.C.   **F5**

Are you ready for a good time?

Gtr Solo

‖: **D5 C5 D5** | **F5 C5 G5** :‖ *play 4 times*

‖: **D5** | **D/F♯** | **G5** | **Fmaj13** :‖

                    D5   **D/F♯**
Chorus 3   Who all need it, who all need it?
                    G5   **F6**
                    You all breathe it, we all breathe it.
                            D5   **C5**   **D5**   **C5**   **G/B**
                    Are you ready for a good time?
                    C5   **G/B**   **D/A**   **G/B**   **C5**   **G/B**
                       Then get ready for the night   line.
                    C5   **D5**   **C5**   **D5**   **F5**   **C5**
                    ‖: Are you ready for a good time?
                    G5   **D5**   **C5**   **D5**
                    Are you ready for a good time?
                    F5   **C5** **G5**   **D5**   **C5**   **D5**   **F5**
                       Are you ready? Are you ready for a good time?   :‖
                    N.C.
                    Are you ready for a good time?

                    | **D5** **F5** **C5** **G5** | **D5**   ‖

Back In Black

Words & Music by
Angus Young and Malcolm Young and Brian Johnson

Intro ‖: **E** **D A** | :‖

Verse 1
    E   **D**
Back in black, I hit the sack,
A
   I've been too long, I'm glad to be back,
       E   **D**
Yes, I'm   let loose from the noose,
A
   That's kept me hangin' about.
     E   **D**   **A**
I keep lookin' at the sky 'cause it's gettin' me high.

Forget the hearse 'cause I never die.
    E   **D**
I got   nine lives, cat's eyes,
   A
Abusin' every one of them and running wild.

Chorus 1
          A E B A   **B**
'Cause I'm back,   yes, I'm back.
A E B A   **B**   **G D G**   **A**
         Well, I'm back,   yes I'm back.
G D A G   **A**   **E B A B A** **E B A**
         Well, I'm back,   back.
      B **G**
Well I'm back in black,
        D
Yes, I'm back in black.

Verse 2

    E   D
Back in the back   of a Cadillac.
    A
    Number one with a bullet, I'm a power pack.
           E   D
Yes, I'm in a bang with a gang,
    A
    They've got to catch me if they want me to hang.
          E   D   A
'Cause I'm back on the track, and I'm beatin' the flack.

Nobody's gonna get me on another rap.
      E   D
So, look at me now, I'm just makin' my play.
        A
Don't try to push your luck, just get outta my way.

Chorus 2

                A E B A   B
'Cause I'm back,   yes, I'm back.
A E B A   B   G D G A
    Well, I'm back,   yes I'm back.
G D A G   A   E B A B A   E B A
    Well, I'm back,   back.
    B G
Well, I'm back in black,
        D
Yes, I'm back in black.

Solo

‖: E   D/E A/E | E |
 | E   D/E A/E | A E A :‖ *play 3 times*
 | E   D/E A/E | E | E   D/E A/C♯ |
 | E   A E A |

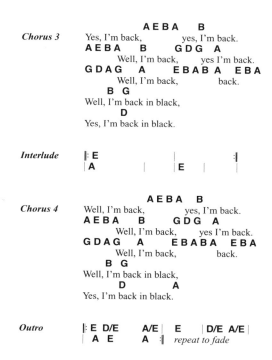

	A E B A	**B**	
Chorus 3	Yes, I'm back,	yes, I'm back.	

A E B A   B   G D G   A
Well, I'm back,   yes I'm back.
G D A G   A   E B A B A   E B A
Well, I'm back,   back.
B G
Well, I'm back in black,
D
Yes, I'm back in black.

Interlude   ‖: **E** | | :‖
                    | **A** | | **E** |

	A E B A	**B**	
Chorus 4	Well, I'm back,	yes, I'm back.	

A E B A   B   G D G   A
Well, I'm back,   yes I'm back.
G D A G   A   E B A B A   E B A
Well, I'm back,   back.
B G
Well, I'm back in black,
D   A
Yes, I'm back in black.

Outro   ‖: **E D/E   A/E** | **E** | **D/E A/E** |
                | **A   E   A** :| *repeat to fade*

Back Seat Confidential

Words & Music by
Angus Young, Malcolm Young and Bon Scott

Intro

```
‖: E5        ‖ Em      |  repeat ad lib.
‖: D           A    | E5  |      :‖  play 4 times
‖: (G)       |      :‖
‖: (E)       |      :‖  play 8 times
```

Verse 1

E5
Old man's car on a Saturday night,
| D5 A5   G5 E5 | G5 E5 |
E5
Got me a woman, me, I feel alright.
| D5 A5   G5 E5 | G5 E5 |
E5
Rock and rollin' at the drive-in show,
| D5 A5   G5 E5 | G5 E5 |
E5
Gonna sit in the back, in the passion row.
| D5 A5   G5 E5 | G5 E5 |
E5
Turn up the soundtrack, turn down the light,
| D5 A5   G5 E5 | G5 E5 |
E5
Chance she won't, but there's a chance she might.
| D5 A5   G5 E5 | G5 E5 |
E5
Ain't no woman in the world I know,
| D5 A5   G5 E5 | G5 E5 |
E5
Ain't had her knickers on the automobile floor.
| D5 A5   G5 E5 | G5 E5 |

Chorus 1

     E5   **D5**
What's that sound? Things goin' down,
A5   **E5**
Look at what's goin' around, back seat confidential.
| **D5 A5** | **D5   A5** | **D5 A5** | **E5** |

Verse 2

E5
Said to buy a rubber at the cigarette stand,
| **D5 A5** | **G5 E5** | **G5 E5** |
E5
Dyin' to get it off so I can get it in.
| **D5 A5** | **G5 E5** | **G5 E5** |
Doin' my best to make a good connection,
E5
She said what are you gonna do 'bout my protection?
| **D5 A5** | **G5 E5** | **G5 E5** |
E5
Alright, mama, gotta listen to me,
E5
Last chance thrill, it's half past three.
| **D5 A5** | **G5 E5** | **G5 E5** |
E5
Huggin' and kissin' would be real nice,
| **D5 A5** | **G5 E5** | **G5 E5** |
E5
Every man's got his price.

Chorus 2

E5   **D5**
What's that sound? Things goin' down.
A5   **E5**
Look at what's goin' around, back seat confidential.

| **(E)** | | | |

Solo

‖: **A** | :‖ *play 4 times*
‖: **B** | :‖ *play 7 times*
| **D5** | | **E5** | |
‖: **N.C.** :‖ *play 3 times*

```
|: E5        |        :| play 14 times
|: A         |        :| play 4 times
|: B         |        :| play 8 times
```

E5

Verse 3   Old man's car on a Saturday night,

| D5 A5   **G5 E5** | **G5 E5** |

E5

Got me a woman, me, I feel alright.

| D5 A5   **G5 E5** | **G5 E5** |

E5

Rockin' and rollin' at the drive-in show,

| D5 A5   **G5 E5** | **G5 E5** |

E5

Gonna sit in the back, in the passion row.

| D5 A5   **G5 E5** | **G5 E5** |

E5

Turn up the soundtrack, turn down the light,

| D5 A5   **G5 E5** | **G5 E5** |

E5

Chance she won't, but there's a chance she might.

| D5 A5   **G5 E5** | **G5 E5** |

E5

Ain't no woman in the world I know,

| D5 A5   **G5 E5** | **G5 E5** |

E5

Ain't had her knickers on the automobile floor.

| D5 A5   **G5 E5** | **G5 E5** |

E5   **D5**

Chorus 3   What's that sound? Things goin' down.

A5

Look at what's goin' around, 'round

E5

Back seat confidential, back seat confidential.

Bad Boy Boogie

Words & Music by
Angus Young, Malcolm Young and Bon Scott

Tune down ½ step:	
6 = E♭	3 = G♭
5 = A♭	2 = B♭
4 = D♭	1 = E♭

Intro
‖: **A5 Asus4 C5/A A5** | **Asus4 C5/A A5** :‖ *play 4 times*
‖: **A5 Asus4 C5/A A5** |
| **Asus4 C5/A A5 Asus4** |
| **C5/A A5 Asus4 C5/A A5** :‖

Verse 1

A5
On the day I was born, the rain fell down.
| **Asus4 C5/A A5** | **Asus4 C5/A A5** |
A5
There was trouble brewing in my home town.
| **Asus4 C5/A A5** | **Asus4 C5/A A5** |
      D5
It was the seventh day, I was the seventh son.
| **Dsus4 F5 D5** | **Dsus4 F5 D5**|
      E   **A5 E5 A**
And it scared the hell out of everyone.

Chorus 1

C5   A5
   They said, "Stop," I said, "Go."
C5   A5
        They said, "Fast," I said, "Slow."
C5   A5
   They said, "Yes," I said, "No."
      C5   A5
I do the bad boy boogie.

Interlude
‖: **A5 Asus4 C5/A A5** |
| **Asus4 C5/A A5 Asus4** |
| **C5/A A5   Asus4 C5/A A5** :‖

A5

Verse 2 Bein' a bad boy, ain't that bad,
| **Asus4 C5/A A5** | **Asus4 C5/A A5** |
A5
I've had me more dirty women,
Than most men ever had.
| **Asus4 C5/A A5** | **Asus4 C5/A A5** |
D5
All you women, come along with me.
| **Dsus4 F5 D5** | **Dsus4 F5 D5** |
E
And I'll show you how good,
A5 E5 A5
A bad boy can be.

C5 A5

Chorus 2 I said, "Right," and they said, "Left."
C5 A5
I said, "East," and they said, "West."
C5 A5
I said, "Up," and they said, "Down."
C5 A5
I do the bad boy boogie, all over town.

Solo ‖: **(C)**   :| **C5 A5** |
play 9 times
‖: **A5**   :| **D5** ‖: **D5**   :| **E5** |
play 7 times   *play 3 times*
‖: **E5**   :| **C5** |
play 3 times
‖: **A5 C5** | **A5 C5** | | :|
play 3 times
| **A5 C5** | **A5 C5** | **A5** | | |
‖: **Asus4 C5/A A5** | **Asus4 C5/A A5** :|
play 4 times

          Asus4   C5/A A5
I wanna tell you no   sto - - - ry,
      Asus4 C5/A A5
Tell you no   lie.
| **Asus4 C5/A A5** |**Asus4 C5/A A5** |
      Asus4 C5/A A5
I was born to   love,   till the day I die.
| **Asus4 C5/A A5** |**Asus4 C5/A A5** |
    D5 G5   **F5 D5**   **G5 F5   D5**
I just line them up,   and I knock them down.
| **G5**   **F5 D5** | **G5 F5 D5** |
        A5 G5 E5
And they all came run - nin',
        A5 G5 E5
When the word got around.
| **A5 G5 E5** | **A5**   **G5 E5 C5**|

  A5

I said, "Up," they said, "Down."
C5   **A5**
   They said, "Straight," I said, "Round,"
C5   **A5**
   They said, "Lost," I said, "Found."
C5 A5
   I said, "Free," and they said, "Bound."
C5 A5   **C5 A5**
Bad boy boogie, do the bad boy boogie.
C5 A5   **C5 A5**
Bad boy boogie, bad boy boogie.

Ballbreaker

Words & Music by
Angus Young and Malcolm Young

Intro	`|Bm A  G |A  G  E |Bm A  G |`
	`|A  G  E5 |   |   |`
	`|: G5  E5  |G5  E5  :|` *play 4 times*

Verse 1

G5 E5   G5 E5
   Breakin' balls,   bangin' walls.
G5 E5   G5   E5
    Work hard and tough,   and I want some rough.
G5 E5   G5   E5
    Unpack my bags,   and take a drag.
G5 E5   G5   E5
    When bang on nine,   and I'm dead on time.

Pre-Chorus

G5   D   A5 E5   G5
      Open up   the door
D   A5 E5   G5
  And lay upon   the floor.
D   A5 E5   G5
  She open her o - - vercoat.
D   G5 D G5 D   G5
  Livin'   out her dreams,
D G5/D D G5/D D
   Rippin' off my   jeans.

Chorus 1

G5 E5   G5 E5   G5 E5
    You are a   ballbreaker.
G5 E
     Ballbreaker.

Verse 2

G5 E5   G5 E5
    Engine roll,   time to go.
G5 E5   G5 E5
    A razorback,   a hog attack.
G5 E5   G5 E5
    We're buildin' steam,   we're whippin' cream.
G5 E5   G5 E5
    She likes a fat,   smokin' stack.

Pre-Chorus

G5 D   A E5   G5
      Hangin' off her legs.

D   A E5   G5
   She threw me on the bed.

D   A E5   G5
   Her hand went for my throat,

D   G5 D G5 D   G5
   As I be - gan   to choke,

D   G5 D   G5 D
   "A-ho - ney shoot your load."

Chorus 2

G5 E5   G5 E5   G5 E5
      You are a   ballbreaker.

G5 E   G5 E
    Ballbreaker,   ballbreaker

Gtr Solo

‖: C5 A5 | C5 A5 | C5 A5 :‖ *play 2 times*
G5 D5 C5	D5 C5 A5
C5 A5	C5 A5
G5 D5 C5	D5 C5 A5
‖: G5 D5	G5 D G5 D :‖ *play 4 times*
‖: Bm A G	A G E5 :‖ *play 4 times*
E	

Chorus 3

G5 E5   G5 E5   G5
      Yeah, Wreckin' ball,   let it roll.

E5   G5 E5   G5
   You are a   ballbreaker.

E5   G5   E5   G5
   Buildin' steam,   we're whippin' cream.

E5   G E
   You are a   ballbreaker.

Pre-Chorus

```
G5 D          A  E5     G5
     Hangin' off her legs.
D               A  E5    G5
  She threw me on the bed.
D               A  E5    G5
  Her hand went for my throat,
D    G5 D  G5 D        G5
  As I be - gan    to choke,
D    G5 D        G5  D
  "A-ho - ney, shoot your load."
```

Chorus 4

```
G5 E5       G5 E5      G5 E5
    You are a    ballbreaker.
G5 E5       G5 E5
    You are a    ballbreaker.
```

Outro

```
‖: G5     E5  | G5     E5   :‖ play 4 times
‖: Bm  A  G   | A   G  E5   :‖ play 8 times
 | Bm  A  G   |
 |            | G5    E5   |
```

24

Beating Around The Bush

Words & Music by
Angus Young, Malcolm Young and Bon Scott

Tune down ½ step:	
6 = E♭	3 = G♭
5 = A♭	2 = B♭
4 = D♭	1 = E♭

Intro   ‖: **(E)** | | | | :‖   *play 5 times*

                     E5   **D5 A5   G5**
Verse 1   Smiling face and lovin' eyes,
                     E5   **D5 A5   G5**
                         But you keep on telling me all those lies.
                     E5   **D5 A5   G5**
                         How do you expect me to believe,
                     E5   **D5 A5   G5**
                         Honey, I ain't that naive.
                     E5   **D5 A5   G5**
                         Baby, I got my eye on you,
                     E5
                          'Cause you do all the things,
                                         D5 A5   G5
                     That I want you to.
                     E5   **D5 A5   G5**
                         Stop your crying and dry your tears,
                     E5   **D5 A5   G5**
                         I ain't that wet behind the ears.

                                       E5
Chorus 1   Well, you can tell me this,
                                   D5
                     And you can tell me lies,
                               A5
                     But where was you last night?
                     E5   **(E)**
                         Beating around the bush.

Verse 2

E5 D5 A5 G5
Wish I knew what's on your mind,
E5 D5 A5 G5
Why you're being so unkind.
E5 D5 A5 G5
Remember those nights we spent alone,
E5 D5 A5 G5
Talking on the telephone?
E5 D5 A5 G5
Thoughts of you go through my brain,
E5 D5 A5 G5
You told me that you felt the same.
E5 D5 A5 G5
It don't seem like you love me too,
E5 D5 A5 G5
Tell me who would lie with you.

Chorus 2

E5
I was talking birds,
D5
You was talking knees,
A5
Or was he down upon his knees,
E5 (E)
Beating around the bush.

Solo

: A5	D5 A5		:
: B5	E5 B5		:
: B5	:	D5	
: E5	:

	E5
Verse 3	You're the meanest woman,

E5

Verse 3 You're the meanest woman,
         D5 A5   G5
I've ever known,
E5   **D5 A5 G5**
   Sticks and stones won't break my bones.
E5   **D5 A5   G5**
I know what you're looking for,
E5   **D5 A5 G5**
   You ate your cake, you want some more.
E5   **D5 A5 G5**
I'm gonna give you just a one more chance,
E5   **D5 A5   G5**
Try to save our romance.
E5   **D5   A5   G5**
   I've done everything I'm gonna do,
E5   **D5 A5   G5**
   The rest is up to you.

                        E5
Chorus 3 You can chew it up,
                        D5
And you can spit it out,
A5
Let it all hang out.
E5   **(E)**
Beating around the bush.

Interlude ‖: **A5** | **D5 A5** | | :‖
             | **A5** | **E5 B5** | |
             | **B5** | **E5 B5** | |

            B5
Chorus 4 Chew it up, spit it out,

Let it all hang out.
D5   **E5**
Beating around the bush.

27

Big Balls

Words & Music by
Angus Young, Malcolm Young and Bon Scott

Intro ‖: E | C :‖ *play 3 times*
         | D | B7

Verse 1
               E   C
Well, I'm rather upper class high society,
      E   C
God's gift to ballroom notoriety.
     E
And I always fill my ballroom,
  C
The event is never small.
   D
The social pages say I've got,
   B7
The biggest balls of all.

Chorus 1
  E   C#m
I've got big balls, I've got big balls,
     E   C#m
They're such big balls, and they're dirty big balls.
   E   C#m
And he's got big balls, and she's got big balls,
  C5   D5   A5   B5
But we've got the biggest balls of them all.

Verse 2

    E   **C**
And my balls are always bouncing,
    E   **C**
My ballroom always full,
      E   **C**
And everybody comes and comes again.
      E
If your name is on the guest list,
    D
No one can take you higher.
B7
Everybody says I've got, great balls of fire.

Chorus 2

E   **C♯m**
I've got big balls, I've got big balls,
      E   **C♯m**
They're such big balls, and they're dirty big balls.
      E   **C♯m**
And he's got big balls, and she's got big balls,
    C5   **D5**   **A5**   **B5**
But we've got the biggest balls of them all.

Verse 3

E
Some balls are held for charity,
    C
And some for fancy dress.
    E
But when they're held for pleasure,
C
They're the balls that I like best.
    E
My balls are always bouncing,
C
To the left and to the right.
    D
It's my belief that my big balls,
      B7
Should be held every night.

	E		C#m
Chorus 3	We've got big balls, we've got big balls,		
	E		C#m
	We've got big balls, dirty big balls.		
	E		C#m
	He's got big balls, she's got big balls,		
	C5	D5 A5	B5
	But we've got the biggest balls of them all.		

Outro   ‖: **E** | **C#m**   :‖
             | **E** | ‖

Breaking The Rules

Words & Music by
Angus Young and Malcolm Young and Brian Johnson

Intro
| A D/A | A | D/A | A G5 |
| A D/A | A | D/A |
| A G5 Dadd11/F♯ E5 |

Verse 1

A/C♯   C5
    Black sheep and a renegade,
G/B   B♭5
    Hot feet in the cool of the shade.
A/C♯   C5
    Street jungle and the tough town hoods,
G/B   B♭5
    Examinations done no good.
A/C♯   C5
    Ghetto bars and a hot wired cars,
G/B   B♭5
    Sneak thieves and cheap cigars.
A/C♯   C5
    No rebellion, not today,
G/B   B♭5 B♭sus4
    I get my kicks in my   own way.
B♭5
Right, ok.

Chorus 1

    A D/A
‖: Just keep on breaking the rules,
A   G   Dadd11/F♯
Come on, get ready to rule.   :‖

Verse 2

A/C♯   C5
    Tough breaks in the neighborhood,
G/B   B♭5
    A hard case who's up to no good.
A/C♯   C5
Living like trash, a society rash,
G/B   B♭5
Ready to break, and ready to dash.
A/C♯   C5
    A bad deal and a real rough ride,
G/B   B♭5
      You're doing time on the other side.
A/C♯   C5
    No rebellion, not today,
G/B   B♭5   B♭sus4
I get my kicks in my   own way.
B♭5
Right, ok.

Chorus 2

  A   D/A
‖:   Just keep on breaking the rules,
A   G   Dadd11/F♯
Come on, get ready to rule.   :‖

Solo

A/C♯ C5	G/B B♭5	A/C♯ C5
G/B	B♭5 B♭sus4	B♭5
‖: A D/A	A G5 Dadd11/F♯ :‖

Verse 3

                    A   D/A
They got reg - ulation ties,
A   D/A
Reg - ulation shoes,
                    A   D/A
Those reg - ulation fools,
                       A   D/A
With their reg - ulation rules.

Chorus 3

              A   D/A
‖:   Just keep on breaking the rules,
A   G   Dadd11/F♯
Come on, get ready to rule.   :‖ *play 4 times*
        G5   Dadd11/F♯   G5   Dadd11/F♯
Get ready,   get ready,
E5   **A/C♯**
          Ready to rule.

Outro   ‖: **A/C♯ C5** | **G/B B♭5** :‖ *repeat to fade w/vocal ad lib.*

Burnin' Alive

Words & Music by
Angus Young and Malcolm Young

Intro

```
|: C#5      |  A5  E5  |          |  B5  C#5 :| play 4 times
|  C#5      |  A5  E5  | E        |  A5  C#5  |
|  C#5      |  A5  E5  | E        |      B5   |
```

Verse 1

C#5
Burnin' alive, set my soul on fire.

Runnin' with a gun, this place is gonna burn.

Pre-Chorus

C# B   F#5 E
   No firewater,   or novacaine.
C# B   F# E5
   No thunderstorm,   no John Wayne.
C#m B   F# E
    No kids to rock,   nowhere to run,

| C#5 C#m B E5 |

F#5   E5
   So watch out 'cause this place is gonna burn.

Chorus 1

      C# A5   E5
Burnin' alive,   burnin' alive.
B5   C# A5   E5
   Burnin' alive,   burnin' alive.
B5   C#
   Burnin' alive,
B5   E5   C#5 B5 E5
   Burnin' alive.

Verse 2

   C#5
They be smokin' your hide, come runnin' wild.

Tell you nothin' to fear, cause the buck stops here.

Pre-Chorus

C♯ B   F♯ E

    No firewater,   or novacaine.

C♯ B   F♯ E5

    No thunderstorm,   no John Wayne.

C♯m B   F♯ E

     No kids to rock,   nowhere to run,

| C♯5 C♯m B E5 |

F♯5   E5

    So watch out 'cause this place is gonna burn.

Chorus 2

         C♯ A5   E5

Burnin' alive,   burnin' alive.

B5   C♯ A5   E5

    Burnin' alive,   burnin' alive.

B5   C♯

    Burnin' alive,

B5   C♯5 B5   A5 E

    It's an all out war, an all out war.

B5   C♯ A   E   B

    Burnin' alive,   burning alive.

Bridge

C♯5   B5 E5 C♯5

Somewhere,   there's a little town called Hope.

B5 E5   C♯5   B

    And someday, maybe baby,

E5   B5   E5

    He'll inhale that smoke, ha ha!

Solo

| C♯5   A5 | B5 | F♯5 | |
| C♯5   A5 | B5 | | |

                       C♯ A5   **E5**

Chorus 3   ‖: Burnin' alive,   burnin' alive.

B5   **C♯ A5**   **E5 B5**

     Burnin' alive,   burnin' alive.   :‖

B5   **C♯5**   **E5**   **C♯**

    It's an all out war,   an all out war.

B5   **E5**   **C♯5**

    Hear the battle roar,

B5   **E5**   **C♯**

    It's an all out war.

                C♯ A5   **E5**

Burnin' alive,   burnin' alive.

B5   **C♯ A5**   **E5 C♯**

    Burnin' alive,   burnin' alive.

B   **E5** **B5**   **C♯**

Outro   Yeah, watch the place burn down.

Can't Stand Still

Words & Music by
Angus Young and Malcolm Young

Intro

‖: **B7** | | ‖
‖: **E5** **Asus4/E A/E** ‖ **B7** |
| **F♯7** | **E7** | **B7** |

Verse 1

B7
When I see a pretty woman,

You know it give me a thrill.
    E5   **Asus4/E A/E**
And she's tailor made to or– – – – – der,
E5   **Asus4/E A/E B7**
  You know I can't stand still.
  F♯7
And you won't need a doctor.
F♯7   **B7**
  'Cause it'll cure all ills.

Verse 2

And when I hear a noisy party,

You know it gives me a chill.
     E5   **Asus4/E A/E**
It gets me rockin' and a roll - - - - -in',
E5   **Asus4/E A/E B7**
  And I can't stand still.
  F♯7
From morning 'til midnight,
E7   **B7**
  You know I can't stand still.

Chorus 1   You know I can't stand still,

I can't stand still.
E7
You know I can't stand still,
B7
I can't stand still.

     F#7
From morning 'til midnight,
E7   **B7**
     You know I can't stand still.

Solo | **B7** | | | | |
                | **E7** | | **B7** | | |
                | **F#7** | **E7** | **B7** | | |

Verse 3   Well, when it comes to sippin' honey,

You know I drink my fill.
        E5   **Asus4/E** **A/E**
And I'll be dancin' on the wa– – – – –ter,
E5   **Asus4/E** **A/E** **B7**
    You know I can't   stand still.
     F#7
From morning 'til midnight,
E7   **B7**
     You know I can't stand still.

Chorus 2 ‖: You know I can't stand still,

I can't stand still.
E7
You know I can't stand still,
B7
I can't stand still.

F♯7
From morning 'til midnight,
E7   **B7**
    You know I can't stand still. :‖

Outro ‖ **B B/A E/G♯ G7** ‖ **B5/F♯ C7 B7** ‖

39

Can't Stop Rock 'n' Roll

Words & Music by
Angus Young and Malcolm Young

Intro	|A G D C |A5 C5 |A5 | |
	|: A5 G5 | D5 :| *play 4 times*
	|A G D C |

Verse 1

```
A C                        A G D C
    Don't you give me no line,
A C                    A G D C
    Better run if you can.
A C                        A G D C
    Just like a thorn in my side,
A C
    So don't give me no.
```

Pre-Chorus

```
F
    Don't you give me no,
A
    Don't you give me no,
F                       D5
    Don't you give me no lies.
```

Chorus 1

```
        A       G5        D
You can't stop rock 'n' roll.
        A       G5        D
You can't stop rock 'n' roll.
```

\|A G D C \|

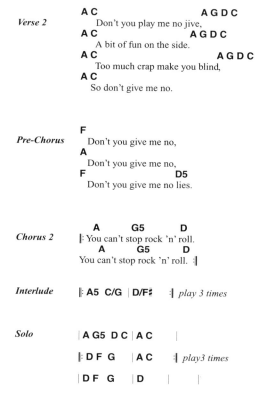

Verse 2

A C   **A G D C**
Don't you play me no jive,
A C   **A G D C**
A bit of fun on the side.
A C   **A G D C**
Too much crap make you blind,
A C
So don't give me no.

Pre-Chorus

F
Don't you give me no,
A
Don't you give me no,
F   **D5**
Don't you give me no lies.

Chorus 2

      A   **G5**   **D**
‖ You can't stop rock 'n' roll.
      A   **G5**   **D**
You can't stop rock 'n' roll. ‖

Interlude

‖ **A5 C/G** | **D/F♯**   ‖ *play 3 times*

Solo

| **A G5 D C** | **A C** |

‖ **D F G** | **A C** ‖ *play3 times*

| **D F G** | **D** | |

Chorus 3

      A   **G5**   **D**
‖: You can't stop rock 'n' roll.
      A   **G5**   **D**
You can't stop rock 'n' roll. :‖

Outro

A **G** **D/F♯**
‖:Ah, ah, ah :‖
      A   **G**   **D**
‖: You can't stop rock 'n' roll :‖
        A   **G**   **D**   **C A5**
I said, you can't stop rock 'n' roll

You can't stop rock 'n' roll.

Caught With Your Pants Down

Words & Music by
Angus Young and Malcolm Young

Intro
‖: **E/G♯ A5 A♯°** | **E5/B A5 G♯5 G5** :‖ *play 3 times*
| **E5 Bm E5 B♭ E5 A** | **E5 G** | **E5** |
‖: **A G5 E5** | :‖ *play 3 times*

Verse 1

　　　　　　　　　　　　　　　　　　　A G5
Runnin' 'round with the wrong crowd,
E5　　　　　　　　　　　　**A G5**
　Goin' out on a last stand.
E5　　　　　　　　　　　　　**A G5**
　Playin' too hard and too loud,
E5　　　　　　　　　　　**A G5**
　Bad cards in a bad hand.
E5　　　　　**A G5 E5**　　　　　**A G5**
　Wanna dance,　　　　wanna sing,
E5
　Whip you with that lickin' thing.

Pre-Chorus

G5　　　　　　　　　　　**A5**
　Tonight I'm gonna kick up,

　Out drivin' in a big truck,

　And maybe I'll get beat up.

Chorus 1

Caught with your pants down.
‖: **B5 B♭5 A5 G♯5 G5 E5** |
E5
Caught with your pants down. :‖ *play 3 times*

| **Bm B♭ A** | **G5 E5** | **A5 G5 E5 E** |

| | **E**   **A5 G♯5 G5** |
| **Verse 2** | Lining up for a roll call, |

E   **A5 G♯5 G5**
Verse 2   Lining up for a roll call,
E   **A5 G5 E5**
Goin' out with a big bang.
E   **A5 G♯5 G5**
Gettin' caught in a shootout,
E   **E/G♯ A5**
Take it hard like a big man.
A♯°   **E5**   **A** **G** **E5 E/G♯**
Woman workin' so hot,
A♯°   **E5**   **A5 E/G♯ A5**
Givin' it everything you've got,
A♯°   **E5**   **A G A5**
Just like it's never gonna stop.

G5   **A5**
Pre-Chorus   Tonight I'm gonna kick up,

Out drivin' in a big truck,

And maybe I'll get beat up.

Chorus 2   Caught with your pants down.
‖: **B5 B♭5 A5 G♯5 G5 E5** |
E5   **(B5)**
Caught with your pants down. :‖ *play 3 times*

                                A
Bridge   She take 'em down, down, down.

                She rip off her stockings,

                When the place started rockin'.
                B
                Down, down, down.

                She was a woman with a mission,
                                        E5
                Stick it in your face.

Solo   ‖: **E5 A5 G5 E5**   :‖ *play 3 times*
                | **E5** |
                | **A5** | | |
                | **E5** | | |
                | **A5** | | **Em**   **E♭ D** | **C**   **A** |
                | **B5** | | |
                | **(B)** | | | **E5**|

                                        A5
Pre-Chorus   Caught with your pants down.

                Down, down, down, down, down.

Chorus 3   ‖: **B5 B♭5 A5 G♯5 G5 E5** |
                                E
                Caught with your pants down. :‖
                B
                Yay!

Outro   ‖: **Bm B♭ A** |
                    G   E5
                Caught you with your pants down.
                | **Bm B♭ A** |
                        E5 G   A5   G   E5
                Caught you with your pants down. :‖ *repeat ad lib.*

                                45

Come And Get It

Words & Music by
Angus Young and Malcolm Young

Intro ‖: **C A5** :‖ *play 4 times*

Verse 1

A5   **C A5**
Pickin' up the sleaze in my car.
                        C A5
Hell no distance too far.
                              C A5
Burning down the road in the night.

Don't you scold me or I'll bite.

Pre-Chorus

| **D7 G/D D7 G/D D7** |
                              G/D D7 G/D
These are the finer things in life,
D7   **E7 A/E E7 A/E**
   Don't think you live in paradise.
E7   **D5**
   I got my filly wrapped in red.

Upon my double decker bed.

Chorus 1

             C   A5
If you want it come and get it. (Come and get it)
             C   A5
If you want it come and get it. (Come and get it)
             C   A5
If you want it come and get it. (Come and get it)
             C   A5   **C A5**
If you want it come and get it.

Verse 2

A5   **C A5**

Suckin' up the juice in the bar.
                              C A5

Downin' every shooter so far.
                                    C A5

Checkin' out the girls what a sight.

If you're gonna blow me, do it right.

Pre-Chorus | **D7 G/D D7 G/D D7** |
                                       G/D D7 G/D

These are the finer things in life,
D7   **E7 A/E E7 A/E**

  Don't think you live in paradise.
E7   **D5**

  I got my filly wrapped in red.

Upon my double decker bed.

Chorus 2

        C   **A5**

If you want it come and get it. (Come and get it)
        C   **A5**

If you want it come and get it. (Come and get it)
        C   **A5**

If you want it come and get it. (Come and get it)
        C   **A5 C A5**   **C A5**

If you want it   come and get me, yeah!

Solo | **C A5** | **C A5** | **C A5** | **C A5** |
        | **G E5** | **G E5** | **G E5** | **G E5** |
        | **C A5 C A5** | **C A5 D** | **C A5 C A5** | **C A5 D C** |
        | **C A5 C A5** | **C A5 D** | **D7 G/D D7 G/D D7** |
        | | **E7 A/E E7 A/E E7** | |

Chorus 3

      C **A5** **G** **E5** **C A5**
Said, if you want it come and get it.
     C **A5** **G** **E5** **C** **A5** **C A5**
If you want it come and get it.
    D   **C** **A5**
‖: If you want it, come and get it. :‖ *play 4 times*
    D   **C** **A5** **C** **A5**
  If you want it, if you want it,
      C **A5**   **C** **A5**
If you want it, come and get it.

Danger

Words & Music by
Angus Young, Malcolm Young and Brian Johnson

Intro | **D5** | | |

Verse 1
D   **G5 D5 G5 D Dsus2/4**
  Don't talk to strangers,
D   **G5 D**   **G5 D Dsus2/4**
  Keep away from the danger, yeah, yeah.
D   **G5 D**   **G5 D Dsus2/4**
  Don't talk to strangers who smile.
D   **G5 D**   **G5**
  Keep away from the danger all the time.
D   **Dsus2/4**
  You just keep away!

Interlude ‖: **E5 A/C♯ D5 A/C♯ D5** | **A5**   :‖ *play 4 times*

Verse 2
D   **G5 D G5 D Dsus2/4**
  Red lights are flashin'.
D   **G5 D** **G5 D Dsus2/4**
  There's been a misunderstanding,
D   **G5 D** **G5 D Dsus2/4**
  I'm bruised, broke an' bandaged.
      D   **G5** **D G5 D Dsus2/4**
Through drinkin' all that brandy.
   A5   **D/A**
I was   under the table,
A   **D/A A**
But I came back for more.
D/A A5   **D/A**
  Got to hit that bottle,
A   **D/A A**
But my head hit   the floor.

Chorus 1

        D/A   E5   A/C♯ D5 A/C♯ D5
We're not   danger,   dan– – – –ger,
A5
   Don't talk to strangers.
E5   A/C♯ D5 A/C♯ D5 A5
Danger,   dan– – – –ger, don't you talk.
E5   A/C♯ D5 A/C♯ D5
Danger,   dan– – – –ger,
A5
   Don't talk to strangers.
E5   A/C♯ D5 A/C♯ D5
Danger,   dan– – – ger,
A5
   Don't you talk, keep away!

Verse 3

D   **G5 D G5 D Dsus2/4**
  Red lights still flashin',
D   **G5 D G5 D Dsus2/4**
  People all still dancin' in my head.
D   **G5 D G5 D   Dsus2/4**
  I've done with thinkin' about what to do.
D   **G5 D G5 D Dsus2/4**
  Another night of drinkin',
A5   **D/A**
Just one before I'm through.
A   **D/A**
I was just raisin' hell,
A   **D/A**   **A**
I wasn't doin' no harm.
D/A   **A5**   **D/A**
The cops could not appreciate,
A D/A   A
My natural charm.

          D/A E5   A/C♯ D5 A/C♯ D5

Chorus 2   We're not   danger,   dan– – – –ger,
A5
   Don't talk to strangers.
E5   A/C♯ D5 A/C♯ D5 A5
Danger,   dan– – – –ger, don't you talk.
E5   A/C♯ D5 A/C♯ D5
Danger,   dan– – – –ger,
A5
   Don't talk to strangers.
E5   A/C♯ D5 A/C♯ D5
Danger,   dan– – – –ger,
A5
Yow!
D   G5   D
  Don't talk to strangers.

|**G5 D Dsus2/4 G5** |

Solo   ‖: **D   G5 D** | **G5 D Dsus2/4 G5** :‖
       | **A5 D/A A** | **D/A   A   D/A** |
       | **A5 D/A A** | **D/A   A   G5** |

          E5   A/C♯ D5 A/C♯ D5

Chorus 3 ‖: Danger,   dan– – – –ger,
A5
   Don't talk to strangers.
E5   A/C♯ D5 A/C♯ D5
Danger,   dan– – – –ger,
A5
   Don't you talk!
E5   A/C♯ D5 A/C♯ D5
Danger,   dan– – – –ger,
A5
   Don't talk to strangers.
E5   A/C♯ D5 A/C♯ D5
Danger,   dan– – – –ger,
A5
   Don' t you talk, keep away! :‖

|**A5**   ‖

Dirty Deeds Done Dirt Cheap

Words & Music by
Angus Young, Malcolm Young and Bon Scott

Intro

```
|: E    G5 | E      A5 |
|  E    D/A | E       :| play 4 times
```

Verse 1

   D5   **E**
If you're   havin' trouble with the high school head,

He's givin' you the blues.
D E
     You wanna graduate, but not in his bed,
D E
     Here's whatcha gotta do.
D E
     Pick up the phone, I'm always home,

Call me anytime.
D   E   **D E**   **D**
Just ring: three-six-two-four-three-six-oh,
E   **D E**
  I lead a life of crime.

Chorus 1

A5   **G5 A5**
Dirty deeds, done dirt cheap.
E   **D E**
Dirty deeds, done dirt cheap.
A5   **G5 A5**
Dirty deeds, done dirt cheap.
E
Dirty deeds and they're done dirt cheap.

Dirty deeds and they're done dirt cheap.

Verse 2

D E
You got problems in your life of love,

You got a broken heart.
D E
He's double-dealin' with your best friend,

That's when the teardrops start, well-uh,
D E
Pick up the phone, I'm here alone,

Or make a social call.
D E   **D   E**
Come right in,   forget about him,
D E
We'll have ourselves a ball.

Chorus 2

A5   **G5 A5**
Dirty deeds, done dirt cheap.
E   **D E**
Dirty deeds, done dirt cheap.
A5   **G5 A5**
Dirty deeds, done dirt cheap.
E
Dirty deeds and they're done dirt cheap.

Solo

‖: **B** | **A** :‖ *play 3 times*
 | **B** | **A** |

‖: **E**   **G5** | **E**   **A5** | **E**   **D/A** | **E**   :‖

Verse 3

D E
If you got a lady and you want her gone,

But you ain't got the guts.
D E
   She keeps naggin' at you night 'n' day,

Enough to drive you nuts.
D E
   Pick up the phone, leave her alone,

It's time you made a stand.
D E   **D E**
   For a fee,   I'm happy to be,
D E   **D E**
   Your backdoor man.

Chorus 3

A5   **G5 A5**
Dirty deeds, done dirt cheap.
E   **D E**
Dirty deeds, done dirt cheap.
A5   **G5 A5**
Dirty deeds, done dirt cheap.
E
Dirty deeds and they're done dirt cheap.

Dirty deeds and they're done dirt cheap.

```
           E
Concrete shoes,
G E           A5  E  E    D  E
    Cyanide,    T.N.T. done dirt cheap.
          G E            A5      E
Neckties,       contracts,     high voltage,
       D  E
Done dirt cheap.


Dirty deeds,
G E                    A     E
    They're ready to send him on the cruise,
       D  E
Done dirt cheap.
          G E            A5 E
Dirty deeds,     dirty deeds,    dirty deeds,
       D  E
Done dirt cheap. Yeah!
```

Dirty Eyes

Words & Music by
Angus Young, Malcolm Young and Bon Scott

Intro | (A) |: **A5** | :| *play 6 times*

Verse 1

A5
Honey, yeah honey.

You do it, uh do it good.

Do it all right, every night.

When you turn off the light,

It's outta sight.

Chorus 1

    D5   **E5**
You hypnotize, mesmerize,
        A5   **(G)**
With your dirty eyes,
(F♯) (G) A5   **(G) (F♯)**
    Your dirty eyes,
(G) A5
     Dirty eyes.

| **(G) (F♯) (G)** | **(F♯) (G) (G♯)** |

Verse 2

A5
Breathing, breathin' heavy.

Heavy, heavy breathin'.

Send shivers down my spine.

Makes me so glad that you're mine.

That's what turns me on,

All night long.

	D5 **E5**

Chorus 2   **D5**   **E5**

You hypnotize, mesmerize,

           A5   **(G)**

With your dirty eyes,

(F♯) (G) **A5**   **(G) (F♯)**

     Your dirty eyes,

(G) A5

    Dirty eyes.

| **(G) (F♯) (G)** | **(F♯) (G) (G♯)** |

Solo   ‖: **A5** | :‖ *play 4 times*

          ‖: **D5** | :‖

          ‖: **E5** | :‖

Outro   **N.C.**

Dirty eyes,

   A5

‖: Dirty eyes, dirty eyes. :‖ *repeat ad lib. to fade*

Dog Eat Dog

Words & Music by
Angus Young, Malcolm Young and Bon Scott

Intro ‖: E5 A5 D5 | | | :‖

                    E5   **A5**

Verse 1   Well it's a dog eat dog,
D5 **A5** **E5** **A5**
  Eat cat too.
D5   **A5** **E5** **A5**
So fish eat frog,
D5   **A5 E5 A5 D5**
  And I eat you.
A5   **D5** **G5**
   Businessman, when you make a deal,
D5   **A5**   **D5**   **G5**   **D5**
Do you know who you can trust?
E5   **A5**   **D5**
Do you sign your   life away,
A5   **E5**   **A5**   **D5**
Do you write your name in dust?

                A5   **B5**

Chorus 1 Hey, hey,   hey!
                 A5
Every dog has his day.
          E5 A5
It's a dog eat dog.
D5   **E5 A5 D5**
  Dog eat dog.

                                    E5 A5

Verse 2   Dog eat dog,
                 D5   **A5 E5 A5**
                    Read the news.
                 D5   **A5 E5 A5**
                   Someone win,
                 D5   **A5 E5 A5 D5**
                    Someone lose.
                 A5   **D5 G5**
                    Up's above and down's below,
                 D5   **A5 D5 G5   D5**
                 And limbo's in between.
                 E5   **A5**   **D5**
                 Up you win, down   you lose,
                 A5 E5 A5   **D5**
                 It's anybody's game.

                               A5   **B5**

Chorus 2   Hey, hey,   hey!
                               A5
                 Every dog has his day.
                        E5 A5
                 It's a dog eat dog.
                 D5   **E5 A5 D5**
                    Dog eat dog.

Solo   ‖: **A5** | **D5 A5** :‖: **E5** | **A5**   **E5** :‖
               ‖: **A5** | **D5 A5** :‖
               ‖: **E5 A5 D5** | :‖ **D5** |

	E5 A5
Verse 3	And it's an eye for eye,

                                              E5   A5

Verse 3

And it's an eye for eye,

D5   A5 E5 A5
  Tooth for tooth.

D5 A5 E5 A5
It's a   lie,

D5   A5 E5 A5 D5
  That's the truth.

A5   D5 G5
  See a blind man on the street,

D5   A5   D5   G5 D5
Looking for something free.

E5   A5   D5
Hear the kind man ask   his friends,

A5 E5   A5 D5
"Hey, what's in it for me?"

                    A5   B5

Chorus 3   Hey, hey,   hey!

                          A5
Every dog has his day.

                E5 A5
It's a dog eat dog.

D5   E5 A5 D5
  Dog eat dog.   *repeat chorus to fade*

Down Payment Blues

Words & Music by
Angus Young, Malcolm Young and Bon Scott

Intro

```
           |           E5 | A5   E5 | A5              |           |
           | E5 A5 E5 A5 E5 A5 | E5            |           |
           |: A5        | E5         | A5              | E5      :|
           | B5         | F♯5        | B5              | F♯5     |
           | D5         | A5         |
           |: B E B E B E | B              :|  play 6 times
```

                                          E B   E B E

Verse 1

```
                        E B   E B E
I know that it's e – – vil,
    B                E   B E B E
    I know that it's got to be.
    B                E      B E B E
    I know I ain't doin' much,
    B                        E   B E B E
    Doin' nothin' means a lot to me.
    B                  D5
    Living on a shoe string,
  A5                    A
    A fifty cent millionaire.
  E5            B  E B E B E
    Open to charity,
    B                    E    B E B E
    Rock 'n' roll around with me.
```

Verse 2

```
    B                E   B E B E
    Sitting in my Cadillac,
    B                    E B E B E
    Listening to my radio.
    B                    E B E B E
    Suzy baby get on in,
    B                        E   B E B E
    Tell me where she want to go.
    B                  D5
    I'm living in a nightmare,
```

A5   A
  She's looking like a wet   dream.
E5   B E   B E B E
  I got myself a Cadillac,
B   E B E B E B
  But I can't afford the gaso - line.

             D5
Chorus 1   I've got holes in my shoes,
            A5   B E B E
      And I'm way overdue,
            N.C.
Down payment blues.

Solo	‖: B E B E B E	B	:‖ *play 4 times*
	‖: Dsus4	D	:‖ *play 4 times*
	‖: A5	E5	:‖
	B E B E B E	B	
	B E B E B E		
	‖: Dsus4	D	:‖
	A5	E5	
	A5		
	‖: B5 E/B		:‖ *play 4 times*
	‖: B E B E B E	B	:‖ *play 4 times*

```
                              E  BEBE
Verse 3      Get myself a steady job,
             B            E  BEBE
               Some responsibility.
             B            E    BEBE
               Can't even feed my cat,
             B          E BEBE
               On social security.
             B            E     BEBE
               Hiding from the rent man,
             A5             A
               Oh it makes me want to cry,
             E5                   B  BEBE
               Sheriff knocking on my door,
             B              E      BEBE
               Ain't it funny how the time flies.


             B              E  BEBE
Verse 4        Sitting on my sailing boat,
             B              E  BEBE
               Sipping on my champagne.
             B            E  BEBE
               Suzy baby you're obscene,
             B               E  BEBE
               Say she want to come again.
             B            E  BEBE
               Feeling like a paper cup,
             A5             A
               Floating down a storm   drain.
             E5         E   BEBE
               Got myself a sailing boat,
             B              E  BEBE
               But I can't afford a drop of rain.
```

	D5
Chorus 2	I've got holes in my shoes,
	A5 **B E B E**
	And I'm way overdue,
	N.C.
	Down payment blues.

| **B E B E B E** |

| | **B**   **E B E B E** |
| *Chorus 3* | ‖: Down payment blues,   :‖ *play 3 times* |

	D5
Outro	I've got holes in my shoes,
	A5 **B E B**
	And I'm way overdue,
	E
	I got the down payment blues.

‖: **B7**   :‖ *repeat to fade*

Evil Walks

Words & Music by
Angus Young and Malcolm Young and Brian Johnson

Intro

E5 ‖: E5 | :‖ *play 3 times*
A	G
E D/F♯ G D/A	A
E D/F♯ G D/A	
‖: E   D A | :‖

Verse 1

E   D   A
Black shadow hangin' over your shoulder,
E   D   A
Black mark up against your name.
E   D   A
Your green eyes couldn't get any colder,
E   D   A
There's bad poison running through your vein.

Chorus 1

E D/F♯ G   D/A A
Evil   walks behind you,
E D/F♯ G   D/A A
Evil   sleeps beside   you,
E D/F♯ G   D/A A
Evil   talks around you,
E D/F♯ G   D/A A
Evil   walks behind   you.

Verse 2

E   D   A
Black widow weavin' evil notions,
E   D   A
Dark secrets bein' spun in your web.
E   D   A
     Good men goin' down in your ocean,
E   D   A
They can't swim 'cause they're tied to your bed.

	E D/F♯ G D/A A
Chorus 2	Evil walks behind you,
	E D/F♯ G D/A A
	Evil sleeps beside you,
	E D/F♯ G D/A A
	Evil talks around you,
	E D/F♯ G D/A A
	Evil walks behind you.

| | **E5** |
| *Link* | You just cry wolf. |

I sometimes wonder where you park your broom.
G E   A
  Ah, black widow!

| *Solo* | ‖: **E   A** ‖   **G E** :‖ *play 4 times* |

	A G
Bridge	C'mon weave your web,
	E A G E
	Down in your ocean,
	A G E
	You got 'em tied to your bed.
	A G E
	With your dark, dark secrets,
	A G E A
	And your green, green eyes,
	G E AG
	You're all evil, whoa!

Chorus 3

```
            E               D/A A
            Evil! Walks behind   you,
            E               D/A A
            Evil! Sleeps beside   you,
            E               D/A A
            Evil! Talks around you,
            E               G  D/A A
            Evil! Walks behind   you.
```

Chorus 4

```
            E  D/F♯ G       D/A A
            Evil       walks behind you,
            E  D/F♯ G         D/A A
            Evil       sleeps beside   you,
            E  D/F♯ G     D/A A
            Evil       talks around you,
            E  D/F♯ G         D/A A
            Evil       walks behind   you.
```

Outro

```
            E  D/F♯ G       D/A A
            Evil       walks behind you,
            E  D/F♯ G         D/A A
            Evil       sleeps beside   you,
            E  D/F♯ G     D/A A
            Evil       talks around you,
            E  D/F♯ G     D/A
            Evil       walks,
            A             D A
            You're so bad.
```

Flick Of The Switch

Words & Music by
Angus Young and Malcolm Young and Brian Johnson

Intro
$\|$: **A5 C5 D5** | :$\|$ |
$\|$: **A5 C5 D5** | :$\|$ *play 4 times*

Verse 1

           A5   **C5**   **D5**
Well, there's a love gone   down on mine,
A5   **C5 D5**
   Suicidal   voltage line.
         A5   **C5**   **D5**
She sends signals   outta distress,
A5   **C5**   **D5**
   She   devil, she evil.

She got you reelin' on a rockin' machine.

Chorus 1

       Am   **D5**
With a flick of the switch,
       Am   **D5**   **G5 D**
With a flick of the switch, she blow ya sky high.
       Am   **D5**
With a flick of the switch,
       Am   **D5**   **G5 D G5 D**
With a flick of the switch, she can satis– –fy.

Link
$\|$: **A5 C5 D5** | :$\|$

	A5 **C5** **D5**

Verse 2

                   A5   **C5**   **D5**
She gonna blow you   all sky high,

A5   **C5**   **D5**
   Flash the eye, electrify.

     A5   **C5**   **D5**
A power force   you should feel.

A5   **C5**   **D5**
    She   devil, she evil.

She got ya screamin' on a lightnin' machine.

Chorus 2

          Am   **D5**
With a flick of the switch,

          Am   **D5**   **G5 D**
With a flick of the switch, she blow ya sky high.

          Am   **D5**
With a flick of the switch,

          Am   **D5**   **G5 D**
With a flick of the switch, she can satis– –fy.

          G5   **D**
Give you pain,

G D   **G D**
    Blow your brain.

Solo   ‖: **Am C D** | | **Am C D** | :‖ *play 4 times*
           | **D** | |

(D)
Flick the switch, flick the switch.

		Am D5

Chorus 3

```
               Am                         D5
With a flick of the switch, she'll blow you sky high.
               Am                 D     G5  D
With a flick of the switch, she can satisfy.
               Am                        D
With a flick of the switch, she gonna burn you down.
               Am                 D    G    D
With a flick of the switch, raised to the ground.
               Am                 D
With a flick of the switch,
               Am              D G5 D
With a flick of the switch.
```

Outro

```
Am                              D
Flick of the switch, she gonna give you pain.
Am                         D  G5      D   G D
Flick of the switch, she gonna    blow your brain.
G D                      G D
        Blow your brain.
D Am         C           D              A5
        She gonna put the lights out on you.
```

Fly On The Wall

Words & Music by
Angus Young, Malcolm Young and Brian Johnson

Intro
A5			: A5 G5 D	G5
A G5 D5	G5 A5 :
: A5 G5 D5	G5 A5	G5 D5	G5 A5 :

Verse 1

A5
You can dance through the night,
    G5
Rock 'n' roll music, itchin' to fight.
      A5
Makin' love,   drunk or stoned.
     G5
Lookin' for dollars, get broken-boned.
    A5 G5 D G5   A5 G5
It's a game,   'cos it's too tough to tame.
D G5   A5   G5 D
  Ends up the same,
G5   A5 G5 D G5
   Sweatin' out rain.

Chorus 1

          A5 G   D G5 D   G5
I was trapped   like a fly on the wall.
          A5   G5 D G5 D G5
I was caged   like a   zoo   animal.
D   A5 G5 D G5 D   G5
No escape   from the fate that you make.
          A5   G5 D G5 D   G5
You're a snake, I've had all   I can take.
D   A5 G5 D
  Watch out,
G5
   There's a fly on the wall.

Verse 2

        A5
Take a chance, take a bite.
       G5
Rock 'n' roll devil, take me tonight.
        A5
Like a bitch   makin' heat,
     G5
Beatin' on my chest, lickin' at my feet.
    A5 **G5 D G5**   **A5** **G5**
It's a game,   'cos it's too tough to tame.
D G5   **A5** **G5 D**
  Ends up the same,
G5   **A5** **G5 D G5**
   Sweatin' out rain.

There's a fly on the wall.

Chorus 2

       A5 **G** **D** **G5 D**   **G5**
I was trapped   like a fly on the wall.
         A5   **G5 D** **G5** **D G5**
I was caged   like a   zoo   animal.
D   **A5 G5** **D** **G5 D**   **G5**
No escape   from the fate that you make.
         A5   **G5 D G5 D**   **G5**
You're a snake, I've had all   I can take.
D
  Watch out,

Interlude | **A G5 D** | **G5 A5** | **A G5 D5**| **G5 A5** |

Solo   ‖: **A G5 D** | **G5 A5** :‖ *play 5 times*
          | **G5 D A** | **G5** | | |

Chorus 3

          A5 G D G5 D   G5
‖: I was trapped   like a fly on the wall.
         A5   G5 D G5 D G5
I was caged   like a   zoo   animal.
D   **A5 G5 D G5 D   G5**
No escape   from the fate that you make.
         A5   G5 D G5 D   G5
You're a snake,   I've had all   I can take. :‖

Outro

     | **D** | **A** **G5** |**D5** **G5** |

               A5
There's a fly on the wall!

For Those About To Rock (We Salute You)

Words & Music by
Angus Young and Malcolm Young and Brian Johnson

Intro	‖: B			Bm B5	Bsus4 :‖
	B5		G5	D/F♯ E	
	B5			G5 D/F♯ E	
	B5 B5/A		G5	D/F♯ E5	
	B5 B5/A			G5 D/F♯ E	
	Bsus4			B5 B5/A	G5
	D/F♯ E			B5 B5/A	G5
	D/F♯ E				

```
        B5        B5/A      G5
          We roll tonight,
D/F♯   E                    B5    B5/A   G5 D/F♯  E
          To the guitar bite, yeah, yeah.
```

```
            B          D/A      A
              Stand up and be counted,
            E                        G5   E
            For what you are about to receive.
            B      D/A    A
              We are the dealers,
            E                            G5   E
            We'll give you everything you need.
            B          D/A      A
              Hail, hail to the good times,
            E                        G5
            'Cause rock has got the right of way.
            E     B          D/A  A
              We ain't no legend, ain't no cause,
            E          G5     E
              We're just livin' for today.
```

Verse 1 (label beside first block)

```
            B5      B5/A      G5    D/F♯  E
*Chorus 1*  ‖: For those about to rock, we salute   you. :‖
```

Verse 2

      B   **D/A**   **A**
We rock at dawn on the front line,
    E   **G5**
Like a bolt right out of the blue.
E   **B**   **D/A A**
  The sky's alight with gui - tar bite,
E   **G5**   **E**
  Heads will roll and rock tonight.

Chorus 2

      B5   **B5/A**   **G5** **D/F♯ E**
‖: For those about to rock, we salute   you. :‖ *play 4 times*

Solo

   ‖: **A D/A A** **I G**   **D**   :‖ *play 8 times*

Verse 3

         B   **D/A**   **A**
We're just a battery for hire with a guitar fire,
E   **G5**
  Ready and aimed at you.
E B   **D/A**   **A**
   Pick up your balls and load up your cannon,
    E   **G5**
For a twenty-one gun salute.

Chorus 3

    E   **B5**
    For those about to rock, fire.
G5 **D** **A**
We salute you.
    B5   **G5** **D** **A**
Oh, for those about to rock, we salute you,
B5
Those about to rock, fire.
G5 **D** **A**
We salute you.
B5
Ow! Fire!
G5 D A **B5** **G5 D A**
We salute you,
B5
We salute you.
G5   **D**
  Come on, go!

Chorus 4

    B5   **G5** **D** **E**
‖: For those about to rock, we salute you. :‖ *play 4 times*
    B5   **G5 D A**
‖: Shoot! Shoot!   :‖ *play 3 times*
B5 G5   **D** **A**
   We salute you.
G5 **D** **A**
‖: We salute you. :‖

Outro

| **B5** **A5** | **G5** **D/F♯** | **E** |

The Furor

Words & Music by
Angus Young and Malcolm Young

Intro

D5			Dsus2	
Csus2		Gm	Dsus2 C9	
Gm		D5 C9	Gm		G5	
: D5 Csus2	Gm/B♭ :	*play 3 times*
G5		Fsus2 C/E	

Verse 1

D5   Csus2   Gm/B♭
Kick the dust, wipe the crime from the main street,
D5   Csus2   Gm/B♭
Await the coming of the Lord.
D5   Csus2   Gm/B♭
Hangin' round with them low down and dirties,
G5
Bringing order from the boss.
D5   C9   Gm/B♭
What's the furor 'bout it all?
D5   Csus2   Gm/B♭
Leave you pantin', bust your balls.
D5   Csus2   Gm/B♭
Kicked around, messed about,
           G
Get your hands dirty, on the killin' floor.

Chorus 1

G5   D5 B♭5 C5
I'm your furor.
G5   D5   B♭5 C5
I'm your furor, baby.
G5
Come on, hey!

Interlude | G5 | D5 | | | |

Verse 2

	D5	C9		G5

D5   C9   G5
Frame of mind, cross the line to a new state,
D5 C9   G5
  I can shake the law.
D5   C9   G5
   Find a mine, gonna build me a new place,

I'm not knockin' door to door.

Chorus 2

G5   D5 B♭5 C5
  I'm your furor.
G5   D5   B♭5 C5
  I'm your furor, baby.
G5   D5   B♭5 C5
  A-what's your furor?
G5   D5   B♭5 C5
  I'm your furor, baby.
G5
  Yeah, yeah, yeah!

Interlude   ‖: **D5 F5 G5 D5** | **Fsus4 G5 D5** :‖

Solo | **D5 Csus2** | **Gm/B♭** | **D5   Csus2** | **G5** |
      | **D5 Csus2** | **Gm/B♭** | | **Csus2** |
      | **D5** | | | |

Chorus 3	**G5** **D5 B♭ C**

G5   **D5 B♭ C**

Chorus 3 Well, I'm your furor,

G5   **D5**   **B♭ C**

  What's your furor, baby?

G5   **D5**   **B♭ C**

  Feel the furor,

G5   **D**   **B♭ C**

  I'm the furor, baby.

G5   **D5**

  I'm your furor.

                    B♭ C

What's your furor, baby?

G5   **D5** **B♭ C**

  Feel the furor,

G5   **D5** **B♭ C5 G5**

  You're my furor.

Outro   **‖: D5 F G D5 :‖**

        D5   **F G D5**

  I'm your furor,

F G   **D5**

    I'm your furor!

Get It Hot

Words & Music by
Angus Young, Malcolm Young and Bon Scott

Tune down ½ step:
6 = Eb   3 = Gb
5 = Ab   2 = Bb
4 = Db   1 = Eb

Intro   ‖: **B E/B   B E/B B** | **E/B B E/B B** :‖ *play 4 times*

Verse 1

B
Going out on the town,

Just a me and you.

Gonna have ourselves a party,

Just like we use to do.
E   A   B5
Nobody's   playing Manilow,
E   A   B5
Nobody's playing soul.
E   A   B5
And no one's playing hard to get,
E   A   B5
Just a-good old rock 'n' roll.

Chorus 1

B E/B B
Get it hot,
B E/B B
Get it hot.
B E/B B
Come on baby,
B E/B B
Get it hot.
B E/B B
Get it hot,
B E/B B
Get it hot,

Alright.

Link | **E5   A5 E5 B5** | |

B

Verse 2   Movin' down the motorway,

               Got a whole lotta booze.

               Got myself a sweet little number,

               Who's got nothing to lose.
                      E   **A5**   **B5**
               Gonna bend you like a G string,
               E   **A**   **B5**
               Conduct you like a choir.
                      E   **A**   **B5**
               So get your body in the right place,
                      E   **A**   **B5**
               We'll set the world on fire.

                         B E/B B

Chorus 2   Get it hot,
                         B E/B B
               Get it hot.
                           B E/B B
               Come on baby,
                         B E/B B
               Get it hot.
                         B E/B B
               Get it hot,
                         B E/B B
               Get it hot,

               Alright.

Link | **E5   A5 E5 B5** | |

Solo   ‖: **E   A   B** | **E** :‖ *play 3 times*
               | **E   A   B** |

Chorus 3

       B E/B B
Get it hot,
      B E/B B
Get it hot.
         B E/B B
Come on baby,
      B E/B B
Get it hot.
      B E/B B
Get it hot,
      B E/B B
Get it hot,
         B E/B B
Oh, yes indeed!
      B E/B B
Get it hot,
         B E/B B
Come on baby,
      B E/B B
Get it hot.
            B E/B B
Make me feel good,
      B E/B B
Get it hot.

         B E/B B
Come on baby,
      B E/B B
Get it hot.

Whoa, now!

Outro | **E5 A5 E5 B5** | |

Girls Got Rhythm

Words & Music by
Angus Young, Malcolm Young and Bon Scott

Intro ‖: D5 C5 | A5 | D5 C5 | A5 :‖

Verse 1

                D5   **C5**   **A5**   **D5**   **C5**
I've been around the world, I've seen a million girls.
A5   **D5**   **C5**   **A5**   **D5**   **C5**
Ain't one of them got, what my lady she's got.
A5   **D5**   **C5**   **A5**   **D5**   **C5**
   She stealin' the spotlight, knocks me off my feet.
A5   **D5**   **C5**
She's enough to start a landslide,
A5   **D5**   **C5**
Just a walkin' down the street.
A5   **D5**   **C5**   **D5**
Wearing dresses so tight, and looking dynamite,
C5   **D5**
Enough to blow me out,
B   **E**
No doubt about it, can't live without it.

Chorus 1

       D5   **C5**   **A5**
The girl's got rhythm. (Girl's got rhythm)
       D5   **C5**   **A5**
The girl's got rhythm. (Girl's got rhythm)
       A5   **D5**   **C5**   **A5**
She's got the backseat rhythm. (Backseat rhythm)
       D5   **C5**   **A5**
The girl's got rhythm.

Interlude | D5 C5 | A5 | D5 C5 | A5 |

Verse 2

        A5   D5   C5   A5   D5 C5
          She's like a lethal brand, too much for any man.
        A5   D5   C5 A5   D5   C5
        She gives me first degree, she really satisfies me.
        A5 D5   C5   A5 D5   C5
          Love me till I'm lifeless,   aching and sore.
        A5   D5   C5
          Enough to stop a freight train,
        A5   D5   C5
        Or start the Third World War.
        A5   D5   C5   D5   C5
          You know I'm losin' sleep, but I'm in too deep.
              C5   D5
        Like a body needs blood,
        B   E
        No doubt about it, can't live without it

Chorus 2

            D5   C5   A5
        The girl's got rhythm. (Girl's got rhythm)
            D5   C5   A5
        The girl's got rhythm. (Girl's got rhythm)
            A5   D5   C5   A5
        She's got the backseat rhythm. (Backseat rhythm)
            D5   C5   A5
        The girl's got rhythm.

Solo   ‖: D5 C5 | A5 | D5 C5 | A5 :‖ *play 4 times*

| | **A5**   **D5** |
| | **Bridge** |

Bridge

      A5   **D5**
You know she moves like sin,
C5   **D5**
And when she lets me in,
C5   **D5**   **C5**
It's like liquid love.
D5   **C5**
No doubt about it, can't live without it.

Chorus 3

      D5   **C5**   **A5**
‖: The girl's got rhythm. (Girl's got rhythm)
        D5   **C5**   **A5**
The girl's got rhythm. (Girl's got rhythm)
      A5   **D5**   **C5**   **A5**
She's got the backseat rhythm. (Backseat rhythm)
        D5   **C5**   **A5**
The girl's got rhythm. (Girl's got rhythm) :‖

Give It Up

Words & Music by
Angus Young and Malcolm Young

Intro

‖: **A5 G A5 G** | :‖
‖: **A5 G A5 G** :‖ *play 3 times*

Verse 1

A5   **D5**
There will be no words of fightin',
          A5
Around here.
D5   **A5**
   'Cause nothin' don't matter,
D5   **A5**
'Cause it ain't clear.
 D5   **A5**
   Well it could be on a Monday,
D5   **A5**
   Or it could even be a Sunday.
 D5   **A5**
   So if you can't stand the distance,
D5   **A5**
You better disappear.

Do I make myself clear?

Pre-Chorus

         G5   **D5**
I'm ready to rock,
G5 D5   **G5 D5**
I'm   gonna rip it.
A5   **E5**
Ready to rock,
A5   E5   **A5   E5**
Yeah, I'm gonna stick it.

A5

Chorus 1   Give it up, give it out,

           A5   **D5**

             Whip it out all about.

           D5 **A5**

             Stick it up, shout it loud

           D5   **E5**   **D5 A5**

             Come on, give it up,

            E5   **D5 A5**

          ||: Give it up,   :||

          E5

          Give it up.

          A5   **D5**

Verse 2   There's a big storm a-howlin',

                 A5

          Around here.

          D5   **A5**

            And there be no wine,

          D5   **A5**

          No sinnin', and no beer.

          D5   **A5**

            I'm gonna aim to fire a rocket,

          D5   **A5**

            There ain't no damn way to stop it,

          D5   **A5**

            I got a sure fire bullet,

          D5   **D5**

          To get you outta here.

          Do I make myself clear?

	G5 **D5**
Pre-Chorus	I'm ready to rock,

G5 D5   G5 D5
I'm   gonna rip it.
A5   E5
Ready to rock,
A5   E5   A5   E5
Yeah, I'm gonna stick it.

A5

Chorus 2   Give it up, give it out,
A5   D5
    Whip it out all about.
D5   A5
    Stick it up, shout it loud
D5   E5   D5 A5
   Come on, give it up,
   E5   D5 A5
‖: Give it up,   :‖
E5
Give it up.

D5

Bridge   I'm goin' crazy on a wild man's night,

Take your pick of anything you like.
            A5 D5 C5   A5
Give it up,   give it up.
D5
   Sittin' pretty, all ready to bite,

She's givin' up a bit of cream delight,
            E5 D5 A5 E5
Give it up, give it up.
D5 A5 E5 D5 A5 E5
Give it up, give it   up.

88

A5　　　　　　　**D5**
Chorus 3　　Give it up, give it out,
A5　　　　　　　**D5**
Whip it up all about.
D5　　**A5**　　　　　　　　**D5**
　　You gotta stick it up, shout it loud.
A5　　　　　　**D5**
　　Give it up all around.
A5　　　　　　　**D5**
　　Give it up, give it up, give it up
A5　　　　　**D5**
Givin' it in, givin' it out.
A5　　　　　　　**D5**
Stick it up, stick it up, stick it out.
A5　　　　**D5**
Give it up alright,
　E5　　　　**D5 A5 E5**　　　**D5 A5**
‖: 　Give it up,　　　give it up,　　　　:‖
E5　　　　**D5 A5 E5**　　　　**D5 A5**
Givin' it up,　　　stickin' it up,
E5　　　　**D5 A5 E5**　　　**D5**
Givin' it up,　　　givin' it up.

Give it up.

| **A5 G5 A5 G5** | **D5 G5 D5** |　　**A5**　　‖

Given The Dog A Bone

Words & Music by
Angus Young and Malcolm Young and Brian Johnson

Intro ‖: **A5**   :‖ *play 6 times*

A5

Verse 1 She'll take you down easy,

Going down to the devil,

Down, down to ninety degrees.

Oh, she's blowing me crazy,

Till my ammunition is dry.
                          D5/A   **A5**
Now, she's usin' her head again.
                    D5/A
She's usin' her head.
A5   **D5/A**   **A5**
   Oh, she's using her head again.

                    E5   **A5** **E5** **A5**
Chorus 1 I'm just a-givin' the dog a bone.
            E5   **A5** **E5**
You bet, I'm givin' the dog a bone.
A5   **E5**   **A5** **E5**
   Yes, I'm givin' the dog a bone.
A5   **E5**   **A5** **E5**
   I'm just a-givin' the dog a bone.
A5   **E5**
Givin' the dog a bone.

Link ‖: **A5**   :‖

Verse 2

A5
She's no Mona Lisa,

No, she's no Playboy star.

But she'll send you to heaven,

Then explode you to Mars.
           D5/A   **A5**
Now, she's usin' her head again.
        D5/A
She's usin' her head.
A5   **D5/A**   **A5**
  Oh, she's using her head again.

Chorus 2

          E5   **A5** **E5** **A5**
I'm just a-givin' the dog a bone.
     E5   **A5** **E5**
You bet, I'm givin' the dog a bone.
A5   **E5**   **A5** **E5**
  Yes, I'm givin' the dog a bone.
A5   **E5**   **A5** **E5**
  I'm just a-givin' the dog a bone.
A5   **E5**
Givin' the dog a bone.

Solo

‖: **A5**		**D5 A5** :‖	*play 4 times*
‖: **E5**		**A5 E5** :‖	*play 3 times*
A5 E5		**A5 E5**	
G5 A5 G5		**A5 G5 A5**		

A5

Verse 3   She got the power of union,

Yeah, she only hits when it's hot.

And if she likes what you're doin',

Yeah, she'll give you a lot.

I'm givin' everything I got.

          E5   **A5**   **E5**

Chorus 3   ‖: Givin' the dog a bone
                A5   **E5**
(Givin' the dog a bone) :‖ *play 4 times*
            A5   **D5**   **A5**
‖: I'm just givin' the dog a bone
              D5   **A5**
(Givin' the dog a bone) :‖ *play 3 times*
            C   **D**   **C D**   **C**   **D**   **C**
I'm just a-givin' the dog,   givin' the dog,
D   **C**   **D**
   Givin' the dog,
C G   **D5**   **A5**
   Ooh, I'm just a givin' a dog a bone.

Go Down

Words & Music by
Angus Young, Malcolm Young and Bon Scott

Intro

‖: **A5** | | :‖ *play 4 times*
‖: **A5**   **G5** | **A5**   **G5** :‖

Verse 1

A5
Ruby, Ruby, where you been so long?

I've just been drinking whiskey,

Baby since you been gone.
                  G5 A5
Ain't no one I know, good as, good as you,
G5   A5   **G5**
    Lickin' on that rhythm stick,
A5   **G5**
    The way you do.

| **A5**   **G5** | **A5**   **C5** |

Pre-Chorus

D5   **C5**   **D5**   **C5**
    You got the lips to make a strong man weak,
D5   **C5**
    And a heathen pray.
D5 E5   **D5 E5**   **D5**
    You do it to me in the way you speak,
E5   **D5 E5**   **A5**
    Girl, it's just the way you go down.

Chorus 1

A5
Go down, go down, go down, go down,

Go down, go down, go down, go down.

	A5
Verse 2	Mary, Mary, you're the one for me.

And the way you hum, sting like a bumblebee.

I'll be 'round to see you 'bout,
            G5 A5
'bout half past ten,
G5   A5   **G5   A5   G5**
Ain't felt this good since I don't know when.

| **A5**   **G5** | **A5**   **C5** |

D5   **C5   D5**
Pre-Chorus   You got the touch that I need so much,
C5   D5   **C5**
  In your finger tips.
D5 E5   **D5**   **E5**   **D5**
  I got the honey that you love to taste,
E5   **D5**   **E5**
  On those lovely lips.
        A5
So go down.

        A5
Chorus 2   Go down, go down, go down, baby go down,

Go down, go down, go down, go down.

Solo

‖: **A5**		:‖ *play 7 times*
	D5	**C5 D5**	**C5 D5**	**C5 D5**
	E5	**D5 E5**	**D5 E5**	**D5 E5**
	A5 ‖: **A5**		:‖ *play 7 times*

A5

Verse 3   Oh baby rub it on, it's sticky and sweet,

It's been so long.

And no else got a touch like you,

I let you do things to me,

I let no other women do.

It feels good, it feels good, oh yeah,

You do it like you should.

‖: **A5**   :‖ *play 8 times*

         D5

Outro   Oh, yeah, yeah,
                   E5
I loved you so much.

It makes me glad I'm a man.
         A5
‖: Go down, go down, go down. :‖ *repeat to fade*

Gone Shootin'

Words & Music by
Angus Young, Malcolm Young and Bon Scott

Intro

```
‖: F♯5        |          |          |        :‖
‖: F♯5   E    | B   F♯5 :‖  play 6 times
|        E    |
```

Verse 1

```
B F♯5                 E
   Feel the pressure rise,
B F♯5                 E
   Hear the whistle blow,
B F♯5                  E
   Found a ticket of a roller car,
B F♯5            E
   Gee, I don't know.
B F♯5                  E          B
   Fought so hard in a travelling band,
F♯5               E
  And never said, "Bye-bye."
B F♯5                          E
   Something's missing in the neighborhood,
B F♯5              E B F♯5
  All the cryin' eyes.
C♯5          C♯sus4
  I stirred my coffee with the same spoon,
B5            A5
  Do a fav'rite tune.
```

Chorus 1

```
F♯5          E B F♯5
Gone shootin',
E B    F♯5                  E
   My baby's gone shootin'.

| B    F♯5    |    E |
```

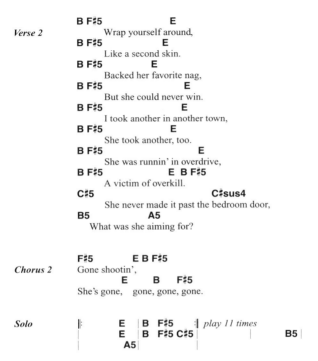

Verse 2

B F♯5   **E**
    Wrap yourself around,
B F♯5   **E**
    Like a second skin.
B F♯5   **E**
    Backed her favorite nag,
B F♯5   **E**
    But she could never win.
B F♯5   **E**
    I took another in another town,
B F♯5   **E**
    She took another, too.
B F♯5   **E**
    She was runnin' in overdrive,
B F♯5   **E B F♯5**
    A victim of overkill.
C♯5   **C♯sus4**
    She never made it past the bedroom door,
B5   **A5**
   What was she aiming for?

Chorus 2

F♯5   **E B F♯5**
Gone shootin',
        E   **B**   **F♯5**
She's gone,   gone, gone, gone.

Solo

‖:   **E** | **B** **F♯5**   :‖ *play 11 times*
 | **E** | **B** **F♯5 C♯5**| | **B5** |
 | **A5**| |

Chorus 3

      F#5   **E**
Gone shootin'.
B   **F#5**
  My baby's gone shootin'.
E   **B**
  Hey look out,   whoo!
F#5
    (Gone shootin'.)
E   **B**
  I might go and get a gun,
F#5
    (Gone shootin'.)
B   **E**   **F#5**
  Wow! Look out! Look out! Look out!

(Gone shootin'.)
E   **B**   **F#5**
I shoot at everyone,

(Gone shootin'.)
E   **B**
Ah, she sure is loaded,
F#5   **E**
    She's gone, gone, gone, gone.
B   **F#5**
  She's gone.
            F#sus4
(Gone shootin'.)

Got You By The Balls

Words & Music by
Angus Young and Malcolm Young

Intro   **A5** ‖: **D5 A5** **C5 A5** | **G5 D5 A5 D5**   **A5** :‖ *play 4 times*

                A5 D5 **A5 C5** **A5 G5 D5 A5**

Verse 1 Hey, Mister Businessman,
              D5   **A5 D5 A5 C5 A5**
      Head of the compa – ny,
G5 D5 A5 D5   **A5 D5 A5 C5 A5**
      Are you looking for a   la – – – dy,
G5 D5 A5 D5   **A5 D5**   **A5 C5 A5 G5 D5**
          One who likes to please?
A5 D5   **A5 D5 A5 C5 A5 G5 D5 A5**
       Hey, Mister Businessman,
              D5   **A5 D5 A5 C5 A5 G5**
     This one likes to   tease,
D5 A5 D5   **A5 D5 A5 C5 A5 G5**
        With her special serv – – ice,
D5 A5 D5   **A5 D5 A5 C5 A5**
      And her French qualit – – ies.

             G5 D5 A5 D5 A5 C5

Pre-Chorus   But she won't sacrifice,
       D5
      What you want tonight.
      C5
      She won't come across,
            D5
      Unless there's money in her hand.
          E5
      And she's calling all the shots.

                              A5   D5 A5 C5 A5
Chorus 1   She got you by the balls.
                  G5 D5 A5 D5   **A5 D5 A5 C5 A5**
                  ‖:   She got you by the balls.   :‖ *play 3 times*
                  G5   D5   A5
                     She got you by the balls, yeah!

                              A5 D5   A5 C5   A5 G5 D5 A5
Verse 2   Hey, Mister Businessman,
                  D5   A5 D5 A5 C5 A5
                     High society,
                  G5 D5 A5 D5   **A5 D5 A5 C5 A5**
                              She can play the school girl,
                  G5 D5 A5 D5   ⁄   **A5 D5 A5 C5 A5**
                     And spank you all you please.

                  G5 D5 A5 D5 A5 C5
Pre-Chorus   But she won't sacrifice,
                  D5
                  What you want tonight.
                  C5
                  She won't come across,
                          D5
                  Unless there's money in her hand.
                      E5
                  She does you all the time.

                              A5   D5 A5 C5 A5
Chorus 2   She got you by the balls.
                  G5 D5 A5 D5   **A5 D5 A5 C5 A5**
                  ‖:   She got you by the balls.   :‖ *play 3 times*
                  G5   D5   A5
                     She got you by the balls, yeah!

| *Interlude* | ‖: **D5 A5 C5 A5** | **D5 A5 C5 A5** :‖ *play 4 times* |

Solo	| **A5 D5 A5** | **D5 A5 D5** | **G5 D5** |
	| **G5 A5 D5** | **A5 D5 A5** | **D5 A5 D5 D/F♯** |
	| **G5 D5** | **G5 A5 D5** |

A5

Bridge   Hang it left, hang it right,

Got you by the balls.
N.C.
Got your shorts, got your curlies,
          A5 D5 A5 C5 A5
Got you by the balls.

G5 D5 A5 D5   **A5 D5 A5 C5 A5**
Chorus 3   She got you by the balls.
          G5 D5 A5 D5   **A5 D5 A5 C5 A5**
‖:   She got you by the balls.   :‖ *repeat ad lib.*

101

Hard As A Rock

Words & Music by
Angus Young and Malcolm Young

Intro
```
‖: B5   E5  B5 |        E5 |     B5 |     :‖ play 4 times
‖: E B5        | E B5      :‖
```

Verse 1

```
E B5            E B5
```
A rollin' rock,   electric shock,
```
E B5              Esus4    E B5
```
  She gives a lickin' that   don't   stop.
```
E B5             E B5
```
  She line 'em up,   push you 'round,
```
E B5                     Esus4 E   B5
```
  Smokin' rings goin' 'round   and 'round.
```
Esus4     B5     Esus4 E
```
     Her hot potatoes,
```
Esus4 E Esus4       B5       Esus4 E Esus4
```
       Will elevate you.
```
Esus4       B5      E Esus4 E
```
     Her bad behavior,
```
        Esus4          B5         E    A5
```
        Will leave you standin' proud.
```
        E5
```
       And hard as a rock.

Chorus 1

```
B5 E B5           E
```
     Hard as a rock,
```
        B5            E
```
Well it's harder than a rock.
```
B5        E
```
Hard as a rock,
```
        B5           B7sus4 E
```
Well it's harder than a rock.

Link

```
| B5      | B7sus4 E |  B5     |
```

E B5   **E B5**
  The lightnin' rod,   strike it hot.
E B5   **Esus4**   **E**
  It's gonna hit you like the   Rushmore rock.
E B5   **E B5**
  No nicotine,   and no pipe dreams,
E B5   **Esus4 E**   **B5**
  So low and dirty it's darn   right mean.
Esus4   **B5**   **Esus4 E Esus4**
     Hell elevator,
E Esus4   **B5**   **E Esus4 E**
  Yeah, I'll see you later.
Esus4   **B5**   **E Esus4 E**
    No, I ain't gonna take it,
Esus4   **B5**   **E A5**
    I'm busting out.
E5
  I'm hard as a rock.

B5 E B5   **E**
     Hard as a rock,
B5   **E**
Harder than a rock.
B   **E**
Hard as a rock,
      B5   **B7sus4 E**
Well it's harder than a rock.
B5 E B5   **B7sus4 E**
    Hard as a rock,
B5   **B7sus4 E**
Harder than a rock.
B5   **B7sus4 E**
Hard as a rock,
B5
Yeah!

| **A5** **E5** **B5** | | **A5** **E5 B5** **E5** | |

Solo |A5 E B5 E | |A5 E B5 E| Esus4 E |
        |A5 E B5 E | Esus4 E A5 | E | |
        |A   E | | | |
        |B5 E5 B5 | E5 | | |

Chorus 3
                    B5
        Well, I'm harder than a rock,
        E5 B5   **E5**
          Hard as a rock,
                    B5
        Baby I'm harder than a rock, yeah!

        B5 E B5   **E**
Outro   Hard as a rock,
                    B5
        Well, it's harder than a rock.
        E B5   **E**
          Hard as a rock,
                    B
        Well, it's harder than a rock.
        E B5   **E**
          Hard as a rock,
                    B5
        Well, it's harder than a rock.
        E B5   **E**
          Hard as a rock.

        Yes I'm harder, harder, harder,
                    B5   **E5 B5**
        Harder than a rock.

Have A Drink On Me

Words & Music by
Angus Young and Malcolm Young and Brian Johnson

Intro

```
|(A)       |          |          |
|: A  D/A  |(A)       :|
```

```
|: A  D/A  |(A)       |          |
| A  D/A   |C C/A C C/A :| play 3 times
```

Verse 1

A
Whiskey, gin and brandy,
    (G)
With a glass I'm pretty handy,
    (D)
I'm try'n' to walk a straight line,
    (A)
On sour mash and cheap wine.
       A5
So join me for a drink boys,
    (G)   G5
We're gonna make a big noise.

Pre-Chorus

     (D)   D5/A
So don't worry about tomorrow, take it today.
D   F   G
Forget about the check, we'll get hell to pay.

Chorus 1

A   D/A (A)   A   D/A
Have a drink on me,   have a drink on me.
C C/A C C/A   D/A
          Yeah, have a drink on me,
(A)   D/A   C C/A
     Have a drink on me.
C C/A
     Come on.

```
|: (A)     |          :|
```

Verse 2

A
Dizzy, drunk and fightin',
    (G)
On tequila white lightnin'.
    (D)
My glass is getting shorter,
    (A)
On whiskey, ice and water.
            A5
So come on and have a good time,
    (G)   **G5**
And get blinded out of your mind.

Pre-Chorus

        (D)   **D5/A**
So don't worry about tomorrow, take it today.
D   **F**   **G**
Forget about the check, we'll get hell to pay.

Chorus 2

A   **D/A (A)**   **A**   **D/A**
Have a drink on me,   have a drink on me.
C C/A C C/A   **D/A**
           Yeah, have a drink on me,
(A)   **D/A** **C C/A**
     Have a drink on me.
C C/A
     Come on.
E5
Get stoned!

Solo

	A5	E5		A5	E5		A5	G	
	D/A			E5	A5 E5		A5	E5	
	A5	E5		E5			A5	E5	
	A5	E5		A5	G				
		D/A						A5	

Chorus 3

    A   **D/A (A)**   **A**   **D/A**
Have a drink on me,   have a drink on me.
C C/A C C/A   **D/A**
              Yeah, have a drink on me,
(A)   **D/A**   **C C/A**
    Have a drink on me.
C C/A
       Come on.

Bridge

    D/A   **G5**   **D/A**
Gonna roll around,   gonna hit the ground.
A5   **G5**   **D/A**
     Take another swig,   have another drink.
A5   **D/A**   **G5**   **D/A**
     Gonna drink it dry,   gonna get me high.
A5   **D/A**   **G5**   **D/A**
     Come on all the boys,   make a noise.

Chorus 4

    A5   **D/A G5**
‖: Have a drink on me,
D/A   **A5**   **D/A**
     Have a drink on me. :‖

Heatseeker

Words & Music by
Angus Young and Malcolm Young and Brian Johnson

Intro

```
| E5        |        |        |        |
|: B5       |        |        |       :|
| A  B  E   |        | A  Bsus4 E |    |
| B         |        |        |        |
```

Verse 1

      E5
Getting ready to rock,

Getting ready to roll,

I'm gonna turn up the heat,

I'm gonna fire up the coal.
     A   **B**   **E**
I gotta keep that motor turning,
     A   **Bsus4 E**
I gotta keep that engine   clean.
     A   **B**   **E**
I gotta keep those tires burning,
       A   **Bsus4 E**
I've got the best you've ever   seen.

Chorus 1

      B5
'Cause I'm a   heatseeker, charging up the sky.

And I'm a heatseeker, and I,
C5 D5   **B5 C5**   **B5**
  I don't need   no life preserver.
C5 D5 B5 C5 D5 B5 C5 D5 B5 A5   **B5**
  I   don't need   no one to hose me down,

To hose me down.

	E5

Verse 2   Ooh, they getting ready to break,

Getting ready to go,

Get your shoes off and shake,

Get your head down and blow.
        A   **B**   **E**
You gotta keep that woman firing,
        A   **Bsus4 E**
You gotta keep that serpent clean,
        A   **B**   **E**
You gotta make her sound the siren,
        A   **Bsus4 E**
You gotta hear that lady   scream.

           B5
Chorus 2   'Cause I'm a   heatseeker, burnin' up the town,

And I'm a heatseeker, and I,
C5 D5   **B5 C5**   **B5**
     I don't need   no life preserver.
C5 D5 B5 C5 **D5** **B5 C5 D5 B5 A5**   **B5**
    I   don't need   no one to hose me down,

To hose me down.

Solo | **B5** | | | **C♯5 D5** |
        | **B5 C♯5 D5** | **B5 C♯5 D5** |
        | **G♯5 A5 C♯5 D5** | **E5** | **D5 E5** |
        | **A5 B5** **D5** **E5** | **C♯5 D5** ‖: **B5 C♯5 D5** :‖ *play 3 times*
        | **D5** | **B5 B5/A B5** | **B5/A B5** |
        | **B5/A B5 B5/A** | **B5 B5/A** | **B5 B5/A B5** |

	B5 **E5**
Verse 3	Here she comes, I wanna see you get up,

And see the whites of your eyes.
         B5
And I'm a   heatseeker, heatseeker.
        E5
I'm gonna measure you up,

I'm gonna try you for size.
        B5
And I'm a   heatseeker.
   A   **B**   **E**
I gotta keep that motor turning,
   A   **Bsus4** **E**
I gotta keep that engine   clean.
   A   **B**   **E**
I gotta keep those tires burning,
      A   **Bsus4 E**
I've got the best you've ever   seen.

	B5
Chorus 3	And I'm a heatseeker, and I,

C5 D5   **B5 C5**   **B5**
    I don't need   no life preserver.
C5 D5 B5 C5 **D5** **B5 C5 D5 B5 A5**   **B5**
    I   don't need   no one to hose me down,

To hose me down,

I'm a heatseeker,

And I'm a heatseeker, heatseeker, ow!

Outro	| **B5** **B5/A B5** | **B5/A B5** | **B5/A B5** |
	| **B5/A B5** |

Hell Ain't A Bad Place To Be

Words & Music by
Angus Young, Malcolm Young and Bon Scott

Intro
‖: **G5 D/F♯ G5** | **G5 D/F♯ G5** | **A** | :‖ *play 4 times*
‖: **A5** | | **G/A A** | **G/A A** :‖

Verse 1

        A5   **G/A A**
Sometimes I think this woman is kinda hot.
G/A A
     Sometimes I think,
                              G/A A
This woman is sometimes not.
G/A A
      Puts me down, fool me around,
G/A A   **G/A A**
    She'd do it to me.

After satisfaction, any diesel action,
  G/A A   **G/A A**
      That ain't the way it should be.
     D/A **Dsus4/A**   **D/A**
She's young, knows I'm the man,
D/A   **Dsus4/A**
    She's gotta see.
D/A   **E**   **A**
'Cause I'm here, it's my year.
E   **G5**
   Brings out the devil in me.

Chorus 1
Hell ain't a bad place to be.
‖: **A** | | **G/A A** | **G/A A** :‖

A

Verse 2   Spends my money, drinks my booze,
G/A A
Stays out every night.
G/A A
But I got to thinking, hey, just a minute,
G/A A
Something ain't right.
G/A A
Hold it, disillusions and confusion,
G/A A   **G/A A**
You make me wanna cry.

Oh, what a shame, you're playing your games,
G/A A   **G/A A**
Tellin' me your lies.
D/A   **Dsus4/A**
Don't mind her playing a demon.
        D/A   **Dsus4/A D/A**
As long as it's with me.
E   **A**
If this is Hell, then you could say,
E   **G5**
It's heavenly.

Chorus 2   Hell ain't a bad place to be.

Solo   ‖: **A5** | | **G/A A** | **G/A A**   :‖ *play 4 times*
         | **G/A A** | **G/A A** |

Verse 3

D/A		Dsus4/A

    Dozens of nights, turns down the lights,

D/A   Dsus4/A D/A

Closes up on me.

E   A

Opens my heart, tears me apart,

E   G5

   She's got the devil in me.

Chorus 3

A   G/A A

Hell, ain't no bad place to be.

  G/A A   G/A A

‖:   I said, hell ain't no bad place to be.   :‖ *play 3 times*

 | **G/A A** | ‖

Hells Bells

Words & Music by
Angus Young and Malcolm Young and Brian Johnson

Intro	‖: **Am Asus4 Am7** | **Asus4 Am** |
	Asus4 Am7 | **A7sus4 C5 G/B Am** :‖
	Asus4 Am7 | **Asus4 Am** |
	Asus4 G | **D C5 G/B A5** | **D5/A** |
	Cadd9 G/B | **A5** **D5/A** | **Cadd9 G/B** |

A5

Verse 1   I'm a rolling thunder,
D5/A   **Cadd9 G/B**
       A pouring rain,
A5   **D5/A**   **Cadd9 G/B**
   I'm comin' on like a   hurricane.
A5   **D5/A**   **Cadd9 G/B**
   My lightning's flashing across the sky,
A5   **D5/A**   **Cadd9 G/B**
   You're only young but you're gonna die.

D5   **C5 G5**
Pre-Chorus   I won't take no prisoners, won't spare no lives.
D5   **C5 G5**
   Nobody's putting up a fight.
E   **D5/A A**
I got my bell, I'm gonna take you to hell.
E5
   I'm gonna get you, Satan get ya.

G5   **Asus4 Am7**
Chorus 1   Hell's bells,
Asus4   **Am**   **Asus4**
       Yeah, hell's bells.
Am7   **A7sus4**   **C5 G/B Am**
   You got me   ringin' hell's bells.
Am7   **Asus4 Am**
My temperature's high.   Hell's bells.

```
|   Asus4  G  |  D   C5 G/B A5 |      D5 |
|   Cadd9 G/B | A5                 D5 |
```

Cadd9   G/B   A5

Verse 2
        I'll give you   black sensations,

D5   **Cadd9 G/B**
Up and down your spine,

A5   **D5**   **Cadd9**
   If you're into evil, you're a friend of mine.

G/B   **A5**   **D5**
   See my white light flashing, as I split the night.

Cadd9   G/B A5
    'Cause if   good's on the left,

   D5   **Cadd9 G/B**
Then I'm stickin' to the right.

D5   **C5 G5**

Pre-Chorus
I won't take no prisoners, won't spare no lives.

D5   **C5 G5**
   Nobody's putting up a fight.

E   **D5/A A**
I got my bell, I'm gonna take you to hell.

E5
   I'm gonna get you, Satan get ya.

G5   **Asus4 Am7**

Chorus 2
   Hell's bells,

Asus4   Am   Asus4
    Yeah, hell's bells.

Am7   **A7sus4   C5 G/B Am**
   You got me   ringin' hell's   bells.

Am7   **Asus4 Am**
My temperature's high.   Hell's bells.

```
|   Asus4  G  |  D   C5 G/B A5 |                |
|  (A)           |                |              |
```
```
```

Solo	‖: **A5 G5 A5** **C5** | **D5** :‖ *play 4 times*
	‖: **D5** | **C5** **G5** :‖ **E** | **D5/A A** |
	| **E** |

G5   **Am Asus4 Am7**   **Am7**

Chorus 3   Hell's bells,   Satan's comin' to you.

Am   **Asus4 Am7**   **A7sus4**

Hell's bells,   he's ringing them now.

C5 G/B   **Asus4 Am7**   **Asus4**

Hell's bells,   the temperature's high.

Am   **Asus4**   **D5**

Hell's bells,   across the sky.

C5 G/B Am Asus4 Am7   **Asus4**

Hell's bells,   they're takin' you down.

Am   **Asus4 C5**   **D5**   **C5**

Hell's bells,   they're draggin' you around.

G/B Am   **Asus4**   **Am7 Asus4**

Hell's bells,   gonna split the night.

Am   **Asus4**   **C5** **D5**

Hell's bells,   there's no way to fight, yeah.

Outro	‖: **A5 G5 A5** **C5** | **D5** :‖ *play 3 times*
	| **A5 G5 A5** | **C5** **D5** |
	| | **A5 G5 A5** |

High Voltage

Words & Music by
Angus Young, Malcolm Young and Bon Scott

Intro

‖: **E**　　**D5** | **A**　　　　:‖ *play 4 times*
| **A**　　　　|　　　　|　　　|　　|

Verse 1

　　　　　　　E　　　　　　　　　　　　　**D5**
Well, you ask me 'bout the clothes I wear,
　　　　　E　　　　　　　　　　　**D5**
And you ask me why I grow my hair,
　　　　　E
And you ask me why I'm in a band.
D5
　　I dig doin' one-night stands.
　　　　　　E
And you wanna see me doin' my thing,
D5　　　　　　　　　　　　　**A**
All you've got to do is plug me in to high,

I said high.

Chorus 1

A5　**C5**　　**D5**　　**A5**
‖: High voltage rock 'n' roll. :‖
C5　**D5**　　　**C5**　**D5**
High voltage, high voltage,
C5　**G5**　　**D**　　**A5**
High voltage rock 'n' roll.

	E **D5**

Verse 2

                    E   **D5**
Well, you ask me why I like to dance,
                 E   **D5**
And you ask me why I like to sing,
                 E
And you ask me why I like to play.
D5
I got to get my kicks someway.
                 E
And you ask me what I'm all about.
D5
C'mon, let me hear you shout.

High, I said high.

Chorus 2

   A5 **C5**   **D5**   **A5**
‖: High voltage rock 'n' roll. :‖
C5 **D5**   **C5** **D5**
High voltage, high voltage,
C5 **G5**   **D**   **A5**
High voltage rock 'n' roll.

Solo

‖: **E**   **D5** | **A** :‖ *play 4 times*
‖: **E** | :‖ *play 4 times*

Chorus 3

   A5 **C5**   **D5**   **A5**
‖: High voltage rock 'n' roll. :‖
C5 **D5**   **C5** **D5**
High voltage, high voltage,
C5 **G5**   **D**   **A5**
High voltage rock 'n' roll.

Outro

‖: **A**   :‖ *repeat to fade*

Highway To Hell

Words & Music by
Angus Young, Malcolm Young and Bon Scott

Intro

| **A** |: **D/F♯ G** | **D/F♯ G** |
| **D/F♯ G D/F♯ A** | :|

Verse 1

  A   **D/F♯ G**   **D/F♯ G**
   Living easy,   livin' free,
D/F♯ G   **D/F♯ A**
Sea - son ticket on a one-way ride.
           D/F♯ G   **D/F♯ G**
Askin' nothin',   leave me be,
D/F♯ G   **D/F♯ A**
Ta– –kin' everythin' in my stride.
          D/F♯ G   **D/F♯ G**
Don't need reason,   don't need rhyme,
D/F♯ G   **D/F♯ A**
Ain't   nothing I'd rather do.
          D/F♯ G   **D/F♯ G**
Going down,   party time,
D/F♯ G   **D/F♯**   **E5**
My   friends are gonna be there too.

Chorus 1

          A   **D/A**
I'm on the highway to hell.
  G   **D/F♯ A**   **D/A**
|: I'm on the highway to hell. :|
  G   **D/F♯ A**   **D/A**
   I'm on the highway to hell.

Verse 2

A   D/F♯ G   D/F♯ G
   No stop signs,   speed limit,
D/F♯ G   D/F♯   A
      Nobody's gonna slow me down.
        D/F♯ G   D/F♯ G
Like a wheel,   gonna spin it,
D/F♯ G D/F♯ A
Nobody's gonna mess me round.
         D/F♯ G   D/F♯ G
Hey Satan,   payin' my dues,
D/F♯ G   D/F♯ A
      Playin' in a rocking band.
        D/F♯ G   D/F♯ G
Hey Momma,   look at me,
D/F♯ G   D/F♯ E5
I'm on my way to the promised land.

Chorus 2

         A   D/A
I'm on the highway to hell.
 G   D/F♯ A   D/A
‖: I'm on the highway to hell. :‖
 G   D/F♯ A   D/A
  I'm on the highway to hell.

| D/A Dsus4/A D/A |

Don't stop me!

| D/A Dsus4/A D/A | Dsus4/A D/A |

Solo   ‖: A   D/A | G D/F♯ :‖ *play 4 times*

Chorus 3

                    A   **D/A**
I'm on the highway to hell.
G   **D/F♯ A**   **D/A**
‖: I'm on the highway to hell. :‖
G   **D/F♯ A**   **D/A**
  I'm on the highway to hell.

Outro

D/A
And I'm going down, all the way.
A
I'm on the highway to hell.

Hold Me Back

Words & Music by
Angus Young and Malcolm Young

Intro	‖: **G** :‖ *play 3 times*	
	G **Csus2**	

Verse 1

     G7   **C**
I got a big fat Cadillac built for you,
                       G7
I got a honk that'll blow the avenue.
                   C
Got a hot dog kickin' all bend my thing,
                               G7
Got a sugar lookin' woman with a bald headed man.
                        C
Give me five oh, here boy, that's what I'll do,
                 G7
Got a big fat mama who can hold a tune.
                 C
Gotta slip that bone in, hard and mean,
                       G5
A honky tonk woman got the best of me.

Chorus 1

               F   **C5**   **G5**
Can't hold me back,   can't hold me back,
                   F
Can't hold me back, get a heart attack,
C5   **G5**
   Can't hold me back.

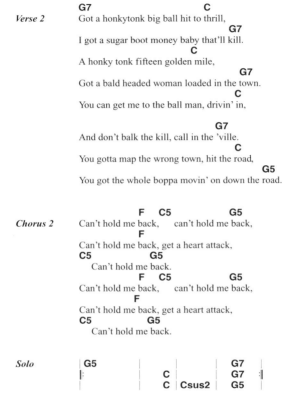

Verse 2

  G7   C
Got a honkytonk big ball hit to thrill,

                                   G7
I got a sugar boot money baby that'll kill.

                     C
A honky tonk fifteen golden mile,

                             G7
Got a bald headed woman loaded in the town.

                         C
You can get me to the ball man, drivin' in,

                        G7
And don't balk the kill, call in the 'ville.

                      C
You gotta map the wrong town, hit the road,

                                  G5
You got the whole boppa movin' on down the road.

Chorus 2

               F   C5   G5
Can't hold me back,   can't hold me back,

               F
Can't hold me back, get a heart attack,

C5   G5
  Can't hold me back.

               F   C5   G5
Can't hold me back,   can't hold me back,

               F
Can't hold me back, get a heart attack,

C5   G5
  Can't hold me back.

Solo

G5			G7	
:		C	G7	:
		C	Csus2	G5	

Chorus 3

                    F   **C5**
You can't hold me back,   you can't hold me back,
                 G5   **F**
You can't hold me back, you can't hold me back,
C5   **G5**   **F**
  Can't hold me back, you can't hold me back.
C5   **G5**
   You can't hold me back, you can't hold me back,
F
 You'll get a heart attack.
C5   **G5**   **Cadd9** **G5**
   Can't hold me back, you can't hold me back,

You can't hold me back.
         Cadd9 **G5**
Can't hold me back, you can't hold me back,
C5
Can't hold me back.
        G5   **C5**   **G5**
You can't hold me back, you can't hold me back.

If You Want Blood
(You've Got It)

Words & Music by
Angus Young, Malcolm Young and Bon Scott

Intro

‖: **A   Asus4 A D**｜ **Dsus4   D** :‖ *play 6 times*
‖: **A** ｜ :‖

Verse 1

    A   **Asus4 A D**
It's criminal,
Dsus4 D   **A**   **Asus4 A D**
     There ought to be   a law,
Dsus4 D A   **Asus4 A D**
      Criminal,
Dsus4 D   **A**   **Asus4 D**
     There ought to be a whole lot more.
Dsus4 D   **A**   **Asus4 A**   **D**
     You get nothin' for no – – – thin',
Dsus4 D   **A**   **Asus4**   **A D**
     Tell me who can you trust?
Dsus4 D A   **Asus4**   **A**   **D Dsus4**
      We got what you want,
D   **A**   **Asus4 A**   **D**
   And you got the lust.

Chorus 1

Dsus4   D   **A**   **G5 D**   **A   G5 D**
‖:   If you want blood,   you got it. :‖
A   **G5 D**
Blood on the streets,   blood on the rocks,
A   **G5 D**
Blood in the gutter,   every last drop.
         A   **G5 D**
You want blood,   you got it.

Yes you have.

‖: **A   Asus4 A D**｜ **Dsus4   D** :‖

	A Asus4 A D
Verse 2	It's animal,

A   **Asus4 A D**
Verse 2   It's animal,
Dsus4 D A   **Asus4 A   D**
             Livin' in a human   zoo.
Dsus4 D A   Asus4 A Dsus4 D
             Animal,
   A   **Asus4 A   Dsus4 D**
The shit that they toss to   you.
A   **Asus4 A D**
Feeling like a Christian,
Dsus4 D A   **Asus4 A D**
             Locked in a cage.
Dsus4 D A   **Asus4 A D**
             Thrown to the lions,
Dsus4 D   A   **Asus4 A D**
             On a second's rage.

Dsus4 D   A   G5 D   A G5 D
Chorus 2   ‖: If you want blood,   you got it.   :‖
A   **G5 D**
Blood on the streets,   blood on the rocks,
A   **G5 D**
Blood in the gutter,   every last drop.
        A   G5 D
You want blood,   you got it.

Yes you have.

Solo | **D** | |
             ‖: **A   Asus4 A D** | **Dsus4   D**   :‖ *play 9 times*
             ‖: **A   Asus4 A D** | **D/F♯   G (C)** |
             | **A   Asus4 A D** | **Dsus4   D**   :‖

126

Chorus 3

```
         A              Asus4   A D
         Blood on the rocks,
         Dsus4 D A              Asus4  A  D/F♯
                  Blood on the streets.
         G      A           Asus4  A D
                  Blood in the sky,
         Dsus4 D A              Asus4  A  D/F♯
                  Blood on the sheets.
         G          A    G5 D
         If you want blood,     you got it!
```

‖: **A   Asus4 A D** | **Dsus4   D** :‖ *play 4 times*

Outro

```
         D            A Asus4 A     D   Dsus4 D
         ‖: If you want blood,     you got it.     :‖ repeat ad lib. to fade
```

Inject The Venom

Words & Music by
Angus Young and Malcolm Young and Brian Johnson

Intro   ‖: **E5 G A   E5** | :‖

Verse 1

G A E5   **G A**
    No mercy for the bad if they want it,
E5   **G A**
Mmm, no mercy for the bad if they plead.
E5   **G A**
  No mercy for the bad if they need it,
E5
Ooh, no mercy from me.
A5 G D   **A   G D**
Tell no truth and   tell no lies,
A5   **G   D**   **A5   G D**
  Cross your heart and   hope to die.
B   **A E**
  Never give what you can't take back,
B   **A E**
  Scratch like   a cat,
B A E
  Inject your venom,
    B   **A   E**
It'll be your last attack.

G A E5   **G A**
No mercy for the bad if they want it,
E5   **G A**
Mmm, no mercy for the bad if they plead.
E5   **G A**
No mercy for the bad if they need it,
E5
V - E - N - O - M.
A5 G D   **A**   **G D**
Got no heart no,   feel no pain.
A5   **G**   **D**   **A5**   **G D**
Take your soul and,   leave a stain.
B   **A**   **E**
Come choose your victim,
B   **A E**
Take him by surprise,
B   **A**   **E**
Go in hard and get him,
     B   **A**   **E**
Right between the eyes.

E5 G5 G♯5   E7   E5
In - ject the venom,
   G5 G♯5 E7   E5
Inject the venom,
             G5 G♯5   E7   E5
Come on, inject the venom,
             E5   G5 G♯5   E7
Come on,   inject it all.
E5   **G A**
Ooh, stick it in,   stick it!

```
||: E5          |  G A   E5 :|  play 3 times
|  E5          ||: A5 G D  | A5 G D    :|
||: B5  A E    |  B5   A E :|
```

Chorus 2	**G5 G♯5 E7 E5**
	Come on, inject the venom,

G5 G♯5   E7   E5
Oh, inject the venom,

A7
Oh, yeah. Oh yeah, oooh yeah, yeah.

E5 G5 G♯5 E7   E5
In - ject the venom,

G5 G♯5 E7   E5
Inject the venom,

G5 G♯5   E7   E5
Come on, inject the venom,

E5   G5 G♯5   E7
Come on,   inject it all.

E5
Ah, inject it all!

It's A Long Way To The Top
(If You Wanna Rock 'n' Roll)

Words & Music by
Angus Young, Malcolm Young and Bon Scott

```
Tune down ½ step:
  6 = E♭   3 = G♭
  5 = A♭   2 = B♭
  4 = D♭   1 = E♭
```

Intro   Bsus4 | B5 | | Bsus4 |
           | B5 | | |
           |: Bsus4 B5 :| *play 9 times*

           Bsus4 B5   Bsus4 B5
Verse 1   Ridin' down the highway,
           Bsus4 B5   Bsus4 B5
                   Goin' to a show.
           Bsus4 B5   Bsus4 B5
                   Stop in all the by–ways,
           Bsus4 B5   Bsus4 B5
                   Playin' rock 'n' roll.
             Bsus4 B5   Bsus4 B5
           Gettin'   robbed, gettin'   stoned.
               Bsus4 B5   Bsus4 B5
           Gettin'   beaten, broken   boned.
               Bsus4 B5   Bsus4 B5
           Gettin'   had, gettin'   took.
           Bsus4 B5
                         I tell you folks, it's harder than it looks.

             Bsus4 B5   A5
Chorus 1   It's a   long way to the top,
                 E/G♯   B
           If you wanna rock 'n' roll.
               B5   A5
           It's a long way to the top,
               E/G♯   B
           If you wanna rock 'n' roll.
           A5/B B
           If you   think it's easy doin' one night stands,
           E/B
                     Try playin' in a rock 'n' roll band.

                      A5   **E/G♯**
                 It's a long way to the top,
                                          B
                 If you wanna rock 'n' roll.

Solo   ‖: **B5** | :‖ *play 4 times*
                 ‖: **B5**   **A5/B B5** | **A5/B B5** :‖
                 | **B5** | | **A5/B** |
                 ‖: **B5**   **A5/B** | **B5 A5/B** :‖ *play 3 times*
                 | **B5** |
                 ‖: **A5**   **E/G♯** | **E5** | **A5/B | B A5/B** :‖ *play 3 times*
                 | **A5** | ‖: **B** | :‖ *play 3 times*

                 B5   **Bsus4 B5**
Verse 2   Hotel, motel,
                 Bsus4 B5   **Bsus4 B5**
                      Makes you wanna cry.
                 Bsus4 B5   **Bsus4 B5**
                      Ladies do the hard sell,
                 Bsus4 B5   **Bsus4 B5**
                      Know the reason why.
                   Bsus4 B5   **Bsus4 B5**
                 Gettin'   old, gettin'   grey.
                   Bsus4 B5   **Bsus4 B5**
                 Gettin' ripped off, under – – – paid.
                    Bsus4 B5   **Bsus4 B5**
                 Gettin'   sold, second   hand.
                    Bsus4 B5
                 That's how it goes, playin' in a band.

Chorus 2   It's a   long way to the top,
                E/G♯   **B**
                If you wanna rock 'n' roll.
                B5   **A5**
                It's a long way to the top,
                E/G♯   **B**
                If you wanna rock 'n' roll.
A5/B B
If you   think it's easy doin' one night stands,
E/B
        Try playin' in a rock 'n' roll band.
        A5   **E/G♯**
It's a long way to the top,
                        B
If you wanna rock 'n' roll.
        Bsus4 B5   **A5**
It's a   long way to the top,
        E/G♯   **B**
If you wanna rock 'n' roll.
B5   **A5**
It's a long way to the top,
        E/G♯   **B**
If you wanna rock 'n' roll.
B5   **A5**
It's a long way to the top,
        E/G♯   **B Bsus4 B5 A5/B B5**
If you wanna rock 'n' roll.
                A5/B B5   **A5/B B5**
Well, it's a   long way
                A5/B B5
It's a   long way, they tell me.
        A5/B B5   **A5/B B5**
It's a   long way,
                A5/B B5
Such a   long way!

Outro   ‖: **B5   A5/B** ‖ **B5   A5/B** :‖ *play 7 times*
                ‖ **B5   A5/B** ‖: **B5**   ‖   :‖ *repeat to fade*

The Jack

Words & Music by
Angus Young, Malcolm Young and Bon Scott

Intro ‖: **B** | **A** :‖ *play 3 times*
         | **E** | **B**

                                             E

Verse 1   She gave me the queen,

She gave me the king,

She was wheelin' and dealin',

Just doin' her thing.
               A
She was holdin' a pair,

But I had to try,

Her Deuce was wild,

But my Ace was high.
  E
But how was I to know,

That she'd been dealt with before,

Said she'd never had a full house.

But I should have known,
         A
From the tattoo on her left leg,

And the garter on her right,

She'd have the card to bring me down,

If she played it right.

E

Chorus 1   She's got the jack,

She's got the jack,

She's got the jack,

She's got the jack,
                    A
She's got the jack,

She's got the jack,
                    E
She's got the jack,

She's got the jack,
                    B
She's got the jack, jack, jack, jack,
A
Jack, jack, jack,
                    E   **B**
She's got the jack.

Solo | **E** | | | |
              | **A** | | **E** | |
              | **B** | **A** | **E** |

              B   **E**
Verse 2   Poker face was her name,

Poker face was her nature,

Poker straight was her game,

If she knew she could get you.
                    A
She play'd 'em fast,

And she play'd 'em hard,

She could close her eyes,

And feel every card.
E
But how was I to know,

That she'd been shuffled before,

Said she'd never had a royal flush.

But I should have known,
A
That all the cards were comin',

From the bottom of the pack,

And if I'd known what she was dealin' out,

I'd have dealt it back.

E
Chorus 2 She's got the jack,

She's got the jack,

She's got the jack,

She's got the jack,
A
She's got the jack,

She's got the jack,
E
She's got the jack,

She's got the jack,
B
She's got the jack, jack, jack, jack,
A
Jack, jack, jack,
E   **B**
She's got the jack.

Chorus 3   **E**
She's got the jack,

She's got the jack,

She's got the jack,

She's got the jack,
     A
She's got the jack,

She's got the jack,
     E
She's got the jack,

She's got the jack,
     B
She's got the jack, jack, jack, jack,
A
Jack, jack, jack,
      E   **F** **E**
She's got the jack.

Jailbreak

Words & Music by
Angus Young, Malcolm Young and Bon Scott

Intro ‖: **E5 D5 A5** :‖ *play 3 times*

Verse 1

E5 D5   A5   E5   D5   A5 E5 D5 A5
   There was a   friend of mine on murder,
E5   D5   A5 E5 D5 A5
   And the judge's gavel fell.
E5   D5 A5   E5
   Jury found him guilty,
D5   A5
   Gave him   sixteen years in hell.
**   E5   D5   A5   E5   D5 A5**
He said,   I ain't spendin' my life   here,
E5   D5 A5   E5 D5
   I ain't livin' alone.
A5   E5   D5   A5   E5   D5
   Ain't breaking no rocks on the chain– –gang,
A5   E5   D5   A5   E5
   I'm breakin' out and   headin' home.
**   D5   A5   E5 A5 A5 E5**
I'm gonna make a jail– – –break.
D5 A5   E5   D5   A5
   And I'm lookin' towards the sky.
E5   D5   A5   E5 D5 A5   E5
   I'm gonna make a jail - - - break.
D5 A5   E5   D5 A5
   Oh, how I wish that I could   fly.

Pre-Chorus

```
A5                        D5  A5 D/A A5
```
All in the name of liberty.
```
B                         E5  B
```
All in the name of liberty.
```
D5
```
Got to be free!

Chorus 1

```
E5  D5 A5  E5   D5  A5
```
Jail– – – – –break,
```
D5      A5  E5  D5 A5
```
Let me outta here!
```
E5  D5 A5  E5
```
Jail – – – – – break,
```
   D5   A5      E5  D5 A5
```
I got to break out,   six - teen years.

```
D5 A5    E5  D5 A5  E5
```
    Hmm, jail– – – – –break,
```
D5 A5    E5          D5
```
Had more than I can take!
```
A5 E5 D5 A5   E5
```
    Jail – – break.

Verse 2

```
D5 A5      E5          D5        A5     E5  D5
```
He said he'd   seen his lady being fooled with,
```
A5 E5       D5  A5 E5 D5 A5
```
        By another man.
```
E5                    D5   A5  E5
```
    She was down and he was up,
```
D5          A5
```
    He had a   gun in his hand.
```
E5          D5   A5  E5  D5 A5
```
Bullets started flying everywhere,
```
E5          D5      A5  E5 D5
```
    And people started to scream.
```
A5    E5      D5   A5       E5
```
    Big man lying   on the ground,
```
D5 A5    E5      E5 A5
```
    With a hole in his body,

                    D5 A5   E5   D5 A5
                    Where his life had   been, but it was.

                    A5   D5 A5 D/A A5
Pre-Chorus   All in the name of liberty.
                    B   E5 B
                    All in the name of liberty.
                    D5
                    Got to be free!

                    E5 D5 A5 E5   D5 A5
Chorus 2   Jail – – – – – break,
                    D5   A5 E5 D5 A5
                    Let me outta here!
                    E5 D5 A5 E5
                    Jail – – – – – break,
                     D5   A5   E5 D5 A5 E5
                    I got to break out,   six – teen years.

                    Outta here.

Solo | **A5** | **D/A** | **A5** | **D/A** |
                    | **B** | **E5** | **B** | **D5** |

Interlude	**E5**
	Heartbeats they were racin',

Freedom he was chasin'.
N.C.
Spotlights, sirens, rifles firing,

But he made it out

With a bullet in his back.

	E5 D5 A5 E5 D5 A5
Outro	‖:Jail - - - - - - break.
	❘ **E5 D5 A5 E5** ❘ **D5 A5** :‖ *repeat to fade*

Kicked In The Teeth

Words & Music by
Angus Young, Malcolm Young and Bon Scott

Verse 1

N.C.   **C5 A5**
Two faced woman with the two faced lies,

                       C5 A5
I hope your two-faced livin' made you satisfied.

             A5
You told me, baby, I was your only one,

While you've been running around town,
          C5 A5
With every mother's son.

Link

C5 ‖: **A5**   **C5** | **A5**   **C5** :‖ *play 3 times*
| **A5**   **C5** | **A5** |

Verse 2

A5
Two times told about the women like you,
C5 | **A5**   **C5** | **A5** |

Two times told about the things you do.
C5 | **A5**   **C5** | **A5** |

I used to think that you were sugar and spice,
C5 | **A5**   **C5** | **A5** |

                    C5 A5
I should've listened to my ma's advice.

Chorus 1   Kicked in the teeth again,
              | **D** | **C G5 D** |
                                              C
              Sometimes you lose, sometimes you win.
              | **A5   C5** | **A5   C5** | **A5   C5** |
              A5
              Kicked in the teeth again,
              | **D** | **C G5 D** |
                                                    E
              Ain't this misery ever gonna end?
                            D
              And I've been   kicked in the teeth,
              C
              Kicked in the teeth again.

Solo   **C5** | **A5   C5** | **A5   C5** | **A5   C5** | **A5** |
              | **D** | **C G5 D** | | **C5** |
              | **A5   C5** | **A5   C5** | **A5   C5** | **A5** |
              | **D** | **C G5 D** | | |
              | **E** | | **D** | **C5** |
              | **A5   C5** | **A5   C5** | **A5   C5** | **A5** |
              ‖: **N.C.** | **C5** | **A5   C5** | **A5** :‖ *play 3 times*
              | **N.C.** | | | **C5** |
              ‖: **A5   C5** | **A5   C5** | **A5   C5** | **A5 C5** :‖

Verse 3

A5
Two faced woman, such a crying shame,
C5 | **A5** **C5** | **A5** |
A
Don't know nothing, you're all the same.
C5 | **A5** **C5** | **A5** |
A
You run around, hope you had your fun,
C5 | **A5** **C5** | **A5** |
A
You never know who's gonna win,
　　　　　　　　C5 A5
Till the race been run.

Chorus 2

Kicked in the teeth again,
| **D** 　　　　　 | 　**C G5 D** |
　　　　　　　　　　　　C5
Sometimes you lose, sometimes you win.
| **A5** **C5** | **A5** **C5** | **A5** **C5** |
A5
Kicked in the teeth again,
| **D** 　　　　　 | 　**C G5 D** |
　　　　　　　　　　　　　　E
Ain't this misery ever gonna end?
　　　D
I've been　 kicked in the teeth,
C　　　　　　　　　**E**
Kicked in the teeth again.

Let Me Put My Love Into You

Words & Music by
Angus Young and Malcolm Young and Brian Johnson

Intro	**Em** ‖: | | **D A5** | **Em** :‖ *play 4 times*

Em
Verse 1   Flying on a free flight,

Driving all night,
         D   **A5**
With my machinery.
Em
'Cause I, I got the power, any hour,
        D   **A5**
To show the man in me.
Em
I got reputations, blown to pieces,
      D   **A5**
With my artillery.
Em
I'll be guidin', we'll be ridin',
         D   **A5**
Givin' what you got to me.

E5   **A5**
Pre-Chorus   Don't you struggle,   don't you fight,
E5   **A5**   **G5 A5**
Don't you worry, 'cause it's your turn to–night.

D5   **A5**   **E5**
Chorus 1   Let me put my love into you, babe.
D5   **A5**   **E5**
Let me put my love on the line.
D5   **A5**   **E5**
Let me put my love into you, babe,
       D5   **A5**   **E5**
Let me cut your cake with my knife.

Link	**Em** | | | **D** **A5** | **Em** |

Em

Verse 2 Oh, like a fever,

Burning faster,
        D   **A5**
You spark the fire in me.
Em
Crazy feelings, got me reeling,
        D   **A5**
They got me raising steam.

      E5   **A5**

Pre-Chorus Don't you struggle,   don't you fight,
      E5   **A5**   **G5 A5**
Don't you worry, 'cause it's your turn to - night.

      D5   **A5**   **E5**

Chorus 2 Let me put my love into you, babe.
      D5   **A5**   **E5**
Let me put my love on the line.
      D5   **A5**   **E5**
Let me put my love into you, babe,
           D5   **A5**   **E5**
Let me cut your cake with my knife.

Solo |: **E5** | **A5** |
   | **E5** | **A5 G5 A5** :| *play 3 times*
   | **E5** | **A5** |
   | **E5** |
   A5
Let me, let me, oh!

Chorus 3

D5   **A5**   **E5**
Let me put my love into you, babe.
D5   **A5**   **E5**
Let me put my love on the line.
D5   **A5**   **E5**
Let me put my love into you, babe,
        D5   **A5**   **E5**
Let me cut your cake with my knife.
D5   **A5**   **E5**
Let me put my love into you, babe.
D5   **A5**   **E5**
Let me put my love on the line.
D5   **A5**   **E5**
Let me put my love into you, babe,
D5   **A5**
  Let me give it all,   let me give it all,
Em
    To you, to you!

freely

Outro | **Em** **D** **A5** | | ‖

Let There Be Rock

Words & Music by
Angus Young, Malcolm Young and Bon Scott

Intro	G5 ‖: E5 G5 │ E5 G5 │ │ E5 A5 E5 G5 │ E5 G5 :‖ *play 4 times*

Link	**(E)** In the beginning, Back in nineteen fifty-five, Man didn't know 'bout a rock 'n' roll show, And all that jive. The white man had the schmaltz, The black man had the blues, No one knew what they was gonna do, But Tchaikovsky had the news. He said "Let there be sound," and there was sound. "Let there be light," and there was light. "Let there be drums," and there was drums. "Let there be guitar," and there was guitar. **A5** Oh, let there be rock.

Bridge	‖: **A5** │ │ │ │ :‖

Solo	‖: **A5**				:‖ *play 3 times*
		B5				
		A5				
	‖:		:‖		
	G5 ‖: **E5**	**G5**	**E5**	**G5**	
		E5 **A5** **E5** **G5**	**E5**	**G5** :‖ *play 4 times*

(E)

Verse 2   And it came to pass.

That rock 'n' roll was born.

All across the land every rockin' band,

Was blowing up a storm.

And the guitarman got famous,

The businessman got rich.

And in every bar there was a super star,

With a seven year itch.

There were fifteen million fingers,

Learning how to play.

And you could hear the fingers pickin',

And this is what they had to say.

Let there be light, sound,

Drums, guitar,
A5
"Oh, let there be rock."

Link   ‖: **A5** | | | :‖

Solo	‖: **A5**				:‖ *play 3 times*
	B5				
	A5				
	‖:		:‖	
	G5 ‖: **E5**	**G5**	**E5**	**G5**	
	E5 A5 E5 G5	**E5**	**G5** :‖ *play 4 times*

          E

Verse 3   One night in a club called The Shaking Hand,
G5 | **E5 A5** | **E5 G5** | **E5** |
E
There was a forty-two decibel rocking band.
G5 | **E5 A5** | **E5 G5** | **E5** |
E
The music was good and the music was loud,
G5 | **E5 A5** | **E5 G5** | **E5** |
E
And the singer turned and he said to the crowd,
G5 | **E5 A5** | **E5 G5** | **E5** |
             A5
"Let there be rock."

Link | **A5** | | | |

Solo   ‖: **A5** | | | :‖ *play 5 times*
        ‖: **B5** | | | :‖ *play 10 times*

freely

| **B** | | | **E** | | |
| **B** | | ‖ | | |

Let's Get It Up

Words & Music by
Angus Young and Malcolm Young and Brian Johnson

Intro
```
| (E)  A D/A |        |
| (E)  A D/A | A      |          |
|: (E)  A D/A |        |
| (E)  A D/A | A      :|
```

Verse 1

A5 B5 E   A5 B5
     Loose lips   sink ships,
A5 B5   E   A5 B5
     So come aboard for a pleasure trip.
A5 B5   E   A5 B5
     It's high tide,   so let's ride,
A5 B5   E   A5 B5
     The moon is risin' and so am I.
         B   E B E
I'm gonna get it up,
B A   B   E B E
     Never gonna let it up.
B A   B   E B E
     Cruisin' on the seven seas,
B A   B E
A pirate of my lovin' needs,
B   A
I'll never go down, never go down.

Chorus 1

     (E)   A D/A
So let's get it up,
       (E)   A D/A A
Let's get it up,
(E)   A D/A
Let's get it up,   right to the top,
     (E)   A D/A A
Let's get it up,   right now.

A5 B5 E   A5 B5

Verse 2   Loose wires   cause fires,

A5 B5   E   A5 B5

Getting tangled in my   desires.

A5 B5   E   A5 B5

So   screw 'em off and   plug 'em in,

A5 B5   E   A5 B5

Then switch it on and start all ov -er again.

B   E B E

I'm gonna get it up,

B A   B   E B E

Never gonna let it up.

A   B   E B E

Ticking like a time bomb,

A   B   E B E

Blowing up the fuse box,

A5

I'll never go down, never go down.

(E)   A D/A

Chorus 2   So let's get it up,

(E)   A D/A A

Let's get it up,

(E)   A D/A

Let's get it up,   right to the top,

(E)   A D/A A

Let's get it up,   right now.

Solo   ‖: **E5** | **D   A**   :‖

‖: **A5 B5 E** | **A5 B5** | **A5 B5 E** | **D   A**   :‖ *play 4 times*

	(E) A D/A
Chorus 3	So let's get it up,
	(E) A D/A A
	Let's get it up,
	(E) A D/A
	Let's get it up,
	(E) A D/A A
	Let's get it up,
	(E) A D/A
	So let's get it up,
	(E) A D/A A
	Let's get it up,
	(E) A D/A
	Let's get it up,
	(E) A D/A A
	Let's get it up.

Outro | **A5** | | **(E)   A D/A** | ‖

Let's Make It

Words & Music by
Angus Young and Malcolm Young

Intro
```
‖: E5        | G5     | D5        | A5        :‖
 | C    F5   | C   G5 | C   F5 G5 | F5 C G5   |
```

Verse 1
```
    C      F5
   Hey sugar baby,
   C        G5
   So hot and tasty,
   C      F5        G5
   Come on and gimme some love,
        F5     C    G5
   You're driving me    wild.
   C      F5    G5
   It's way past midnight,
   C        F5     G5
   Why don't we take a ride.
   C        F5     G5
   We'll make some honey,
        F5   C      G5
   As we cruise real slow.
```

Chorus 1
```
   D    G5  A5
   Let's make it,
   D      G5  A5
   Don't waste it,
   D    G5  A5  D    G5     A5
   Let's make it,   come on and taste it.
   D      G5  A5
   Let's make it,
   D      G5  A5
   Don't waste it,
   D    G5  A5  D    G5     A5
   Let's make it,   come on and taste it.
```

Verse 2

```
C      F5
I'll be your ladies man,
C      G5
If you give me the chance,
C           F5   G5
We keep on jumpin'
        F5    C    G5
'Til the music run   dry.
C    F5    G5
And if we take a rest,
C          F5    G5
We'll smoke some cigarettes,
C          F5    G5
And start a-smoking,
        F5      C/E  G5
Going out of control.
```

Chorus 2

```
D     G5   A5
Let's make it,
D     G5   A5
Don't waste it,
D    G5   A5  D       G5      A5
Let's make it,   come on and taste it.
D     G5   A5
Let's make it,
D     G5   A5
Don't waste it,
D    G5  A5  D       G5      A5
Let's make it,   come on and taste it.
```

Bridge

```
E5              G5
Na-na-na-nah, na-na-na-nah,
D               A5
Na-na-na-nah, na-na-na-nah,
E5              G5
Na-na-na-nah, na-na-na-nah,
D
Na-na-na-nah.
```

```
| A5        |           |           |
```

Solo | C   F5 | C   G5 | C F5 G5 | F5 C G5 |
| C   F5 | C   G5 | C F5 G5 | F5 C/E G5 |
|

D   G5   A5
Chorus 3 Let's make it,
D   G5   A5
Don't waste it,
D   G5   A5 D   G5   A5
Let's make it,   come on and taste it.
D   G5   A5
Let's make it,
D   G5   A5
Don't waste it,
D   G5 A5 D   G5   A5
Let's make it,   come on and taste it.

E5   G5
Bridge Na-na-na-nah, na-na-na-nah,
D   A5
Na-na-na-nah, na-na-na-nah,
E5   G5
Na-na-na-nah, na-na-na-nah,
D
Na-na-na-nah.

| **A5** | |

D   G5   A5
Chorus 4 ‖: Let's make it,
D   G5   A5
Don't waste it,
D   G5 A5 D   G5   A5
Let's make it,   come on and taste it. :‖

Little Lover

Words & Music by
Angus Young, Malcolm Young and Bon Scott

Intro　　　‖: **G5**　　|　　| **Em7**　　|　　　:‖

G5
Verse 1　Saw you in the front row,

Moving to the beat,
Em7
　　　Just movin' and groovin'.
G5
Killed me when I saw,

The wet patch on your seat,
Em7
　　　Was it Coca Cola?

A
Pre-Chorus　Ooh baby, I hope you liked the show,
　　　　　　　C5
When the band said good night,

I had to say hello.

　　　　　(E)　E7♯9
Chorus 1　Little lover,
　　(E)　　　　　**E7♯9　(E)　E7♯9**
　　　I can't get you off my mind, no.
　　(E)　　　　**E7♯9**
　　　Little lover,
　　(E)　　　　　**E7♯9　(E)**
　　　I've been trying hard to find,
　　E7♯9　　　**(E)**
Someone like you.

	G5
Verse 2	Ooh, baby you sure looked sweet,

G5

Verse 2 Ooh, baby you sure looked sweet,
Em7
    Cruisin'.
    G5
A leg either side of my motorcycle seat,
Em7
    Just oozin'.

A

Pre-Chorus Could have been a nightmare,

Could have been a dream,
    C5
But on my way home, baby,

I thought I heard you scream.

            (E) E7♯9
Chorus 2   Little lover,
            (E)   **E7♯9 (E)   E7♯9**
    I can't get you off my mind,
            (E)   **E7♯9**
    Little lover,
            (E)   **E7♯9 (E)**
    Ooh, I tried so hard to find,
    E7♯9 (E)
        Someone to give me the things that I need.

Solo | **G** | | **A** | |
          | **B** | | **C** | **D5 D♯5** |

           (E) E7♯9

Chorus 3   Little lover,

(E)   **E7♯9** **(E)**   **E7♯9**

   I can't get you off my mind,

(E)   **E7♯9**

 No, little lover,

(E)   **E7♯9** **(E)**

   I've been trying hard to find,

E7♯9   **(E)**

Someone like you.

G5

Verse 3   You had my picture,

On your bedroom wall,

Em7

   Next to Gary Glitter, yeah.

   G5

I was standing on the stage,

Playing rock 'n' roll,

Em7

   I was a guitar picker.

A

Pre-Chorus   Never had a record,

Never had a hit,

C5

   Ooh, baby you didn't mind a bit.

	(E) E7♯9

Chorus 4 Little lover,
(E)   **E7♯9   (E)   E7♯9**
  I can't get you off my mind, no.
(E)   **E7♯9**
  Little lover,
(E)   **E7♯9   (E)**
  I've been trying hard to find,
E7♯9   **(E)**
Someone like you, you, you,

Baby, I know you're a…
G5
Little lover,
Em7
Ooh.

Outro   ‖: **G5** | | **Em7** | :‖   *repeat to fade*

Live Wire

Words & Music by
Angus Young, Malcolm Young and Bon Scott

Intro

```
‖: (B)            |        |        |    A5 |
‖:       E    | B5 |        |    A5 :‖  play 3 times
         E    | B5 |        |  E B5 |
‖:            |  E B5 :‖ play 3 times
‖:            | A5 E B5 :‖ play 4 times
```

Verse 1

B5   A5 E
Well, if you're lookin' for trouble,
B5   A5 E
   I'm the man to see.
B5   A5 E
If you're lookin' for satisfaction,
B5   A5 E
I'm satisfaction guaranteed.
B5   E5 B5   A5 E
   I'm as cool as a body on ice,
B5   E   B5   A5 E
   Or hotter than the rollin' dice.
B5   E
   Send you to heaven,
B5   A5 E
   Take you to hell,
B5   E
   I ain't foolin'.
B5
Can't you tell?

Chorus 1

        G5
I'm a live wire, live wire,
       B5
I'm a live wire, live wire
      G5
I'm a live wire, live wire.
F♯5
   Gonna set this town on fire.

| *Link* | ‖: **B5** | **A5 E B5** :‖   *play 4 times* |

      B5   **A5 E**

Verse 2   And if you need some lovin'
      B5   **A5 E**
    And if you need some man.
      B5   **A5 E**
You've got the phone and the number,
      B5   **A5 E**
    And I got no future plans.
      B5   **E** **B5**   **A5**   **E**
   Oh, come on honey, you got nothin' to lose.
      B5   **E** **B5**   **A5 E**
You got the thirst, and I got the booze.
      B5   **E**
   Give you an inch,
      B5   **A5**   **E**
   Take you a mile.
      B5   **E** **B5**
   I wanna make you smile.

          G5

Chorus 2   I'm a live wire, live wire,
        B5
I'm a live wire, live wire,
         G5
I'm a live wire, live wire.
      F♯5
   Holy smoke and sweet desire.

| *Link* | ‖: **(B)** | :‖ *play 4 times* |

Solo   ‖: **B5**   **D5 B5** | **D5 B5** :‖ *play 3 times*
                | **B5**   **D5 B5** | **D5** |
                | **G5** | **B5** |
                | **G5** | **F♯5** | **A5 E B5** |
                ‖: **B5** | **A5 E B5** :‖ *play 3 times*
                | **B5** | | |
                | | | **A5 E B5** |
                ‖: **B5** | **A5 E B5** :‖ *play 4 times*

                B5   **E**   **B5**   **A5 E**

Verse 3   Cooler than a body on ice,
                B5   **E**   **B5**   **A5 E**
                  Hotter than the rollin' dice.
                B5   **E B5**   **A5 E**
                  Wilder than a drunken fight,
                B5   **E**   **B5**
                  You're gonna burn tonight.

                G5

Chorus 3   I'm a live wire, live wire,
                     B5
                I'm a live wire, live wire
                     G5
                I'm a live wire, live wire.
                F♯5
                     I'm gonna set this town on fire.
                G5
                Live wire, live wire,
                     B5
                I'm a live wire, live wire
                     G5
                I'm a live wire, live wire.
                     B5
                I'm a live wire, live wire.

Outro   ‖: **G5** | | **B5** | :‖ *repeat to fade*

Love At First Feel

Words & Music by
Angus Young, Malcolm Young and Bon Scott

Intro
    ‖: **A5**   **G5** | **D**   **A5** :‖ *play 3 times*
    | **A5** | **G5 D E5** |

Verse 1

E
You never told me where you came from,
D
  You never told me your name,
E
  I didn't know if you were legal tender,
    D
But I'd spend it just the same.
E
And I didn't know it could happen to me,
D
  But I fell in love in the first degree.

Chorus 1

    A5   **G5 D**
It was love at first feel.
A5   **G5 D**
Love at first feel,
A5   **G5 D**
Love at first feel.
A5   **G5 D/F♯**
First touch was too much.

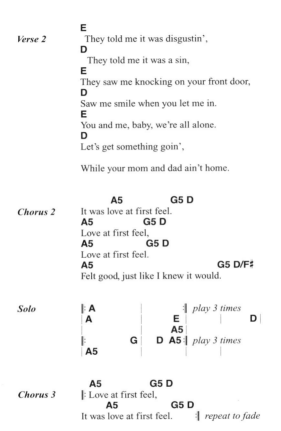

Verse 2

   E
  They told me it was disgustin',
D
  They told me it was a sin,
E
They saw me knocking on your front door,
D
Saw me smile when you let me in.
E
You and me, baby, we're all alone.
D
Let's get something goin',

While your mom and dad ain't home.

Chorus 2

       A5   **G5 D**
It was love at first feel.
A5   **G5 D**
Love at first feel,
A5   **G5 D**
Love at first feel.
A5   **G5 D/F♯**
Felt good, just like I knew it would.

Solo

‖: **A** | :‖ *play 3 times*
 A | **E** | | **D** |
             A5 |
‖:   **G**   **D A5** :‖ *play 3 times*
 A5

Chorus 3

   A5   **G5 D**
‖: Love at first feel,
     A5   **G5 D**
It was love at first feel.   :‖ *repeat to fade*

Love Hungry Man

Words & Music by
Angus Young and Malcolm Young and Brian Johnson

```
Tune down ½ step:
6 = E♭   3 = G♭
5 = A♭   2 = B♭
4 = D♭   1 = E♭
```

Intro   ‖: D | D/F♯ G5 | A5 | :‖ *play 4 times*

Verse 1

D   D/F♯   G5 A5
You're the one I've waited for,
D   D/F♯ G5   A5
I need your lovin' more and more

I don't know what your name is,

I don't know what your game is,

I want to take you tonight,

Animal appetite.

Chorus 1

      D D/F♯ G5 A5
'Cause I'm a love hun–gry man
      D D/F♯ G5 A5
Yeah I'm a love hun–gry man.

Pre-Chorus

G5 A5   G5 A5
   Don't want no conversa – tion,
G5 A5   G5 A5
   I need sweet sensation.
G5 A5   G5 A5
   And all I wanna do,
G5 A5   G5 A5
   Is make a meal out of you.

| | D   D/F♯ G5   A5   G5 A5 |
| *Chorus 2* | 'Cause I'm a love hun – gry man |

        G5 A5
I'm out to get what I can

       D   D/F♯ G5 A5 G5 A5
'Cause I'm a love hun - gry man

       G5 A5
I'm telling you,   that I am.

Solo
```
‖: D    G D |    G D | A5    G5 A5 |   G5 A5 :‖
 |  C   F C | G C G/B | D      G  D |   G D |
 |  C   F C | G C G/B | A      D  A |   D A |
 | A   D  A |           |
```

| | D   D/F♯ G5 A5 |
| *Chorus 3* | I'm your love hun - gry man, |

Oh baby you're such a treat,

D D/F♯ G5 A5
Love hun - gry man,

And a man's got to eat.

    D   D/F♯ G5 A5
I'm a love, you're the one I've waited for,

Oh yes you are.

    D   D/F♯ G5   A5
I'm a love, I need your lovin' more and more,

Yeah, I do.

      D D/F♯ G5   A5 G5 A5
'Cause I'm a love, love   hungry man.

     G5 A5
Oh yes I am,

     D D/F♯ G5   A5 G5 A5
I'm a love, love   hungry man.

        G5 A5
   Just a little bit.

Outro

     D D/F♯ G5 A5 G5 A5

Oh, I'm a love, love hungry man,

G5 A5   **D** **D/F♯ G5** **A5 G5 A5**

‖:   Oh, I'm a love, love hungry man,   :‖ *play 3 times*

Solo

‖: **D** | **D/F♯ G5** | **A5 G5 A5** | **G5 A5**:‖ *w/vocal ad lib.*

| **D** | **D/F♯ G5** |

A5   **A5 G5 A5**

Ooh, love hungry man.

Meltdown

Words & Music by
Angus Young and Malcolm Young

Intro

|: **E7**   **A** | :|
|: **E7**   **A/E** | **E7**   **A/E**   :|

Verse 1

   E7   **A/E**
I look at my watch to find out,
   E7   **A/E**
The right time of day.
   E7   **A/E**
I look at her libido,
E7   **A/E**
Hey, hey, hey.
   E7   **A/E**
I gotta get up and climb her,
E7   **A/E**
Roll her on the hay.
E7   **A/E**
Makin' a sweat, temperature rise,
E7   **A/E**
All through the day.

Pre-Chorus

D   **G**   **D G**
Man it's gettin' hot, hot,   hot.
     D   **G**   **D G**
I said man it's gettin' hot, hot,   hot.
         D   **G**   **D**   **G**
It's getting hotter   and hotter.
D   **G**   **D G**
Man, it's getting hot, hot,
             A5
Getting hot around here.

		E7	A/E E7
Chorus 1	It's a meltdown.		

E7   **A/E E7**

Chorus 1   It's a meltdown.

A/E   **E7**   **A/E E7 A/E**

     It's a meltdown.

         E7   **A/E**

Verse 2   I got a feelin' in my bones,

       E7   **A/E**

I been rackin' my brains out.

E7 A/E E7 A/E

All night long,

E7   **A/E**

Stokin' up the fire.

       E7   **A/E**

Take it right up to the wire.

       E7   **A/E**   **E7 A/E**

Burnin on and on, burnin' on.

D   **G**   **D G**

Pre-Chorus   Man it's gettin' hot, hot,   hot.

      D   **G**   **D G**

I said man it's gettin' hot, hot,   hot.

       D   **G**   **D**   **G**

It's getting hotter   and hotter.

D   **G**   **D G**

Man, it's getting hot, hot,

          A5

Getting hot around here.

       E7   **A/E E7**

Chorus 2   It's a meltdown.

A/E   **E7**   **A/E E7 A/E**

     It's a meltdown.

       E7   **A/E E7**

It's a meltdown.

A/E   **E7**   **A/E**

     It's a meltdown.

E7   **A/E**

     In my brain.

Solo
| A   D/A | A   D/A | E7   A/E | E7   A/E |
| D   G | A5 |: E7   A/E | E7   A/E :|

Pre-Chorus

D   G   D G
Man it's gettin' hot, hot,   hot.
          D   G   D G
I said man it's gettin' hot, hot,   hot.
                  D   G   D   G
It's getting hotter   and hotter.
D   G   D G
Man, it's getting hot, hot,
                        A5
Getting hot around here.

Chorus 3

          E7   A/E E7
|: It's a meltdown.
A/E   E7   A/E E7 A/E
    It's a meltdown.   :| *play 3 times*
        E7   A/E E7
It's a meltdown.
A/E   E5
    It's a meltdown.

freely

|: E5 | :|

Moneytalks

Words & Music by
Angus Young and Malcolm Young

Intro ‖: **G Csus2** | :‖ *play 3 times*
        | **G   D5** | ‖: **G5** | :‖

G5

Verse 1 Tailored suits, chauffered cars,

Fine hotels and big cigars.

Up for grabs, up for a price,

Where the red hot girls keep on dancing,

Through the night.
        D5
The claim is on you, the sights are on me,

So what do you do, that's guaranteed.
        C5
Hey little girl, you want it all,

The furs, the diamonds, the paintings on the wall.

G   **C5**
Chorus 1 Come on, come on, love me for the money.
G   **D5**
Come on, come on, listen to the moneytalk.
G   **C5**
Come on, come on, love me for the money.
G   **D5**
Come on, come on, listen to the moneytalk.

Link ‖: **G5** | :‖

Verse 2

G5
A French maid, foreign chef,

A big house, with king size bed.

You had enough, you ship them out,

The dollar's up, down, you'd better buy the pound.
D5
The claim is on you, the sights are on me,

So what do you do, that's guaranteed.
C5
Hey little girl, you broke the laws,

You hustle, you deal, you steal from us all.

Chorus 2

G   **C5**
Come on, come on, love me for the money.
G   **D5**
Come on, come on, listen to the moneytalk.
G   **C5**
Come on, come on, love me for the money.
G   **D5**
Come on, come on, listen to the moneytalk.

Link   ‖: **D5** | :‖

Solo   ‖: **G5** | :‖ *play 4 times*
             ‖: **D5** | :‖
             ‖: **C5** | :‖

173

```
G Csus2          G
        Money talks,
Csus2      G
        B.S. walks,
Csus2        G
        Money talks,
Csus2
        Come on, come on.
```

```
              G                 C5
Chorus 3      |: Come on, come on, love me for the money.
              G                 D5
              Come on, come on, listen to the moneytalk.
              G                 C5
              Come on, come on, love me for the money.
              G                 D5
              Come on, come on, listen to the moneytalk. :|
```

```
Outro        | G5      |       |       |       ‖
```

Nervous Shakedown

Words & Music by
Angus Young, Malcolm Young and Brian Johnson

Intro | A6 E D | Cadd9 G/B A5 | G5 G5/F♯ E5 |
          ‖: E5   A | G D A5 E5 :‖

Verse 1

E5   **A G D A5**
"Freeze!" said the man cruisin' the beat.
E5   **A G D A5**
You get your hands up, and spread your feet.
E5   **A G D A5**
   "Don't you move an inch, I heard him say."
E5
"Or you'll be doin' time,
                          A G D
Un - til the judgement day."
A5   **A5 A5/C D5**
And he said,
(A)   **A5 A5/C D5**
"Don't tell me no lies, give me alibis,
(A)
'Cause if you cross my path,
                          B5 B5/A D5 A5
You'll be doin' life."
B5   **B5/A D5**
It's a dirty lie.

A5 B5 E5

Chorus 1   It's a shake - down.

A   **G**   **D**   **A5**

And it's a nervous shakedown.

E5

A ner - vous shake - down.

A   **G**   **D**   **A5**

Another nervous shakedown.

E5

Well, it's a shakedown.

A   **G**   **D**   **A5**

And it's a nervous shakedown.

E5

We got a shake - down.

A   **G**   **D**   **A5**

Another nervous shakedown.

Link   ‖: **A6 E D** | **Cadd9 G/B A** :‖

E5

Verse 2   "Take a dime," said the man,

                 A G D A5

"You can make one call."

E5   **A G**

 "You got a one-way ticket to the County Hall."

D A5 E5

      Well, the judge looked high,

           A G D5 A5

And I looked low.

E5

And when he smiled at me,

            A G D5

It was a one-man show.

    A5 C5/A D5

He said,

(A)   **A5 C5/A D5**

"Two to five, the jury decides."

(A)   **B5 B5/A D5 A5**
"Double parole if you survive."
B5   B5/A D5
It's a dirty lie.

                     A5 B5 E5
Chorus 2   It's a shake – down.
A   G   D   A5
And it's a nervous shakedown.
E5
A ner - vous shake – down.
A   G   D   A5
Another nervous shakedown.
E5
Well, it's a   shake – down.
A   G   D   A5
And it's a nervous shakedown.
E5
We got a shake – down.
A   G   D   A5
Another nervous shakedown.

Link | **A6 E D** | **Cadd9 G/B A5** | **G5 G5/F♯ E5** |

Solo   ‖: **E5   A** | **G D A5 E5** :‖ *play 3 times*
                | **E5   A** | **G D A5** |
                ‖: **A5 A5/C D5** | **(A)**   :‖
                ‖: **B5 B5/A D5 A5 B5** :‖

Night Prowler

Words & Music by
Angus Young, Malcolm Young and Bon Scott

Tune down ½ step:
6 = E♭	3 = G♭
5 = A♭	2 = B♭
4 = D♭	1 = E♭

Intro   ‖: **A5 D5** | **Csus2 D5** :‖
       | **D5** | |
       ‖: **A5 D5** | **Csus2 D5** :‖ *play 4 times*
       ‖: **A5 D5** | **G5 D5** :‖

Verse 1
                    A5   **D**   **G D**
          Somewhere a clock strikes midnight,
                         A5   **D**   **G D**
          And there's a full moon in the sky.
                              A5   **D G D**
          You hear a dog bark in the distance,
                         A5   **D G D**
          You hear someone's baby cry.
               A5   **D**
          A rat runs down the alley,
                    G   **D**
          And a chill runs down your spine.
                    A5   **D**
          And someone walks across your grave,
                    G   **D**
          And you wish the sun would shine.
                         A5   **D**
          'Cause no one's gonna warn you,
                    G   **D**
          And no one's gonna yell attack.
                    A5   **D**
          And you don't feel the steel,
                    G   **D**
          Till it's hangin' out your back.

	A5 D5 Csus2 D5
Chorus 1	I'm your night prowler, I sleep in the day.

Chorus 1

        A5 D5   **Csus2**   **D5**
I'm your night prowler, I sleep in the day.
        A5 D5   **Csus2 D5**
I'm your night prowler, get out of my way.
            A5 D5   **Csus2**   **D5**
Look out for the night prowler, watch you tonight.
        A5 D5   **Csus2**   **D5**
I'm the night prowler, when you turn out the light.

Solo   ‖: **A5 D5** | **Csus2 D5** :‖ *play 4 times*

Verse 2

        A5   **A6**
Too scared to turn your light out,
            A7   **A6**
'Cos there's something on your mind.
        A5   **A6**
Was that a noise outside your window,
            A7   **A6**
What's that shadow on the blind?
        A5   **A6**
As you lie there naked,
        A7   **A6**
Like a body in a tomb.
        A5   **A6**
Suspended animation,
        A7   **A6**
As I slip into your room.

Chorus 2

        A5 D5   **Csus2**   **D5**
I'm your night prowler, I sleep in the day.
        A5 D5   **Csus2**   **D5**
I'm your night prowler, get out of my way.
            A5 D5   **Csus2**   **D5**
Look out for the night prowler, watch you tonight.
        A5 D5   **Csus2**   **D5**
I'm the night prowler, when you turn out the light.

| *Solo* | ‖: **A5 D5** | **Csus2 D5** :‖ *play 7 times* |
| | ‖: **A5 D5** | **Csus2** | **D5** |

           A5 D5   **Csus2**   **D5**

Chorus 3   I'm your night prowler, I sleep in the day.

           A5 D5   **Csus2 D5**

I'm your night prowler, get out of my way.

              A5 D5   **Csus2 D5**

Look out for the night prowler, watch you tonight.

           A5 D5   **Csus2**   **D5**

I'm the night prowler, when you turn out the light.

           A5 D5   **Csus2**   **D5**

Outro   I'm your night prowler, break down your door.

           A5 D5   **Csus2**   **D5**

I'm your night prowler, crawling 'cross your floor.

           A5 D5   **Csus2**   **D5**

I'm your night prowler, make a mess of you,

A5   **D5**   **Csus2**

Night prowler, and I am telling this to you.

D5

There ain't nothin',

           A5

Nothin' you can do.

Overdose

Words & Music by
Angus Young, Malcolm Young and Bon Scott

Tune down ½ step:
6 = E♭   3 = G♭
5 = A♭   2 = B♭
4 = D♭   1 = E♭

Intro

‖: B7 | |
   E | :‖ *play 6 times*
‖: B5 D5 E5 B5 | D5 E5 B5 :‖ *play 8 times*

Verse 1

B5 D5   E5   B5   D5 E5
  I never smoked with no cigarettes,
B5 D5   E5   B5   D5 E5
  I never drank much booze.
      B5 D5 E5   B5   D5 E5
But I'm only a   man, don't you understand,
B5   D5   E5   B5 D5 E5
And a man can sometimes lose.
B5   D5   E5   B5   D5 E5
  You gave me something I never had,
B5   D5   E5   B5 D5 E5
  Pulled me down   with you.
B5   D5   E5 B5   D5   E5
  Help me up,   bring on the love.
B5   D5   E5
  Hope you can pull me through.

Chorus 1

B5   E
  I overdosed on you,
D   E
  I overdosed on you.
D   E
  Crazy but it's true,
D   E
  Ain't nothing I can do.
D
I overdosed on you.

| *Link* | ‖: **B5 D5 E5 B5** │ **D5 E5 B5** :‖ *play 4 times* |

	B5 D5 E5 B5 D5 E5
Verse 2	Oh, woman you give to me,
	B5 D5 E5 B5 D5 E5
	More than I can take.
	B5 D5 E5 B5 D5 E5
	But listen honey, I don't mind.
	B5 D5 E5 B5 D5 E5
	You're a habit I don't want to break.
	B5 D5 E5 B5 D5 E5
	Don't want none of that hard stuff,
	B5 D5 E5 B5 D5 E5
	Don't need it anymore.
	B5 D5 E5 B5 D5 E5
	I'm in love, and I'm sinking fast,
	B5 D5 E5
	And I don't need no cure.

	B5 E
Chorus 2	I overdosed on you,
	D E
	I overdosed on you.
	D E
	Crazy but it's true,
	D E
	Ain't nothing I can do.
	D
	I overdosed on you.

Solo	‖: **B5 D5 E5 B5** │ **D5 E5 B5** :‖ *play 7 times*
	‖: **B5 D5 E5 B5** │ **E** :‖
	‖: **E** **D** │ **E** :‖ *play 3 times*
	│ **E** │ **D** │
	‖: **B5 D5 E5 B5** │ **D5 E5 B5** :‖ *play 4 times*

	D5 E5 B5 D5 E5
Verse 3	Gee, I was happy as a man could be.
	B5 **D5 E5** **B5 D5 E5**
	Too far gone to save,
	B5 **D5** **E5** **B5 D5 E5**
	Power of love, don't pull me off.
	B5 **D5** **E5** **B5**
	Just write on my grave.

Verse 3

D5 E5   B5   D5 E5

Gee, I was happy as a man could be.

B5   D5 E5   B5 D5 E5

Too far gone to save,

B5   D5   E5   B5 D5 E5

Power of love,   don't pull me off.

B5   D5   E5   B5

Just write on my grave.

Chorus 3

                            E

I overdosed on you,

D   E

I overdosed on you.

D   E

Crazy but it's true,

D   E

Ain't nothing I can do.

D

I overdosed on you.

Outro   ‖: **B7** | **E** | :‖ *play 8 times*
                 | **B7** | | ‖

Problem Child

Words & Music by
Angus Young, Malcolm Young and Bon Scott

Intro   **D5 A5** ‖:   **D5 G5** | **D5 A5** :‖ *play 4 times*

                D5 A5   **D5 G5**

Verse 1   Cop this,   I'm hot,

                        D5 A5   **D5**   **G5 D5**

And when I'm not,   I'm cold as ice.

A5   **D5**

  Get out of my way,

G5   **D5 A5**   **D5 G5**

  Just step aside,   or pay the price.

    D5   **G5**   **D5**   **G5**

What I want I take, what I don't I break.

D5   **G5 D5**

  And I don't want you,

A5   **E5**   **A5 E5**

With a flick of my knife, I can change your life.

A5 E5   **A5 E5**

    There's nothing you can do.

   G5   **A5**   **C5 D5**

Chorus 1   I'm a problem child,

         A5   **C5 D5**

I'm a problem child,   yes I am,

G5   **A5**   **C5 D5**

  I'm a problem child,

A5   **G5 E D5 A5**

  And I'm wild.

Link   ‖: **A5**   **D5 G5** | **D5 A5** :‖

        D5 G5

Verse 2   Make my stand,   no man's land,

       D5 A5 **D5 G5**

        On my own.

       D5 A5   **D5 G5**

        Man in blue, it's up to you,

       D5 A5   **D5 G5**

        The seed is sown.

       G5 **D5**   **G5**   **D5**

       What I want I stash, what I don't I smash.

       G5 D5   **G5 D5**

        And you're on my list.

       A5 E5   **A5 E5**

        Dead or alive, I got a forty five.

       A5 E5   **A5 E5**

        And I never miss.

       G5 **A5**   **C5 D5**

Chorus 2   I'm a problem child,

         A5   **C5 D5**

       I'm a problem child,

       G5 **A5**   **C5 D5**

        I'm a problem child,

       A5   **G5 E**

       Just runnin' wild!

Solo   ‖: **B5** **A5 E5** | :‖ *play 4 times*

      ‖: **A5** **C5 D5** | :‖ *play 3 times*

      | **A5** **G5 E5** |

          D5 A5 ‖: **D5 G5** | **D5 A5** :‖ *play 4 times*

D5 G5

Verse 3   Every night,   street light,
D5 A5   D5 G5
    I drink my booze.
D5 A5   D5 G5
    Some run,   some fight,
D5 A5   D5 G5
    But I win they lose.
D5   G5   D5
What I need I like, what I don't I fight,
G5 D5   G5 D5
    And I don't like you.
A5 E5   A5 E5
    Say bye-bye, while your still alive,
A5 E5   A5 E5
    Your time is through.

G5   A5   C5 D5

Chorus 3   'Cause I'm a problem child
A5   C5 D5
I'm a problem child,
G5   A5   C5 D5
    I'm a problem child,
A5   C5 D5
I'm a problem child,
G5 A5   C5 D5
    Problem child,
A5   C5 D5
I'm a problem child,
A5   C5 D5
I'm a problem child,
A5   C5 D5
I'm a problem child,

A5 B5   D5 E5

Outro   ‖:   Problem child.   :‖ *repeat ad lib. to fade*

Put The Finger On You

Words & Music by
Angus Young and Malcolm Young and Brian Johnson

Intro   ‖: **A5   G5/A D/A** | :‖

Verse 1

A5   **G5/A D/A**
I put the finger on   you, yeah
    A5   **G5/A D/A**
My hands all out of control.
    A5   **G5/A D/A**
Yes and I can't stop it get - tin' down on you,
    A5   **G5/A**   **D/A**
It's moving on its own accord.
B   **E5**
  Yes, I got fire in my finger tips,
B   **E5**
Radiating onto you.
B   **E5**
  I can't control it, can't even hold it,
    B
It's knocking on your door.
    E5
And you know what it's for.

Chorus 1

G D   **G D A/E**   **E**
I put the finger right on you.
G D   **G D A/E**   **E**
I put the finger right on you.
G   D   **G D A/E E**
You put your finger on me too.
G D   **G D G D**   **G D**
I put the finger, I put the finger,
    A E   **A E A E**   **A E**
Yeah, I put the fin–ger, I put the finger.

Verse 2

A5   G5/A D/A
I put the finger on you for sure.
   A5   G5/A D/A
It's the key to unlocking your door, don't you know.
A5   G5/A D/A
I've broken through your security,
  A5   G5/A D/A
My hands ain't tied no more, you better watch out.
B   E5
 I can't control it, can't even hold it.
B   E5
It's sneaking up on your front door,
    B
You can feel it on your ankle.
E5
Feel it on your knee,
B   E5
Feel it on your thigh, can you feel me?

Chorus 2

G D G D A/E E
I put the finger right on you.
G D G D A/E E
I put the finger right on you.
G D   G D A/E E
You put your finger on me too.
G D G D G D G D
I put the finger, I put the finger,
   A E A E A E A E
Yeah, I put the fin - ger, I put the finger.

Solo   ‖: A5 G5/A D/A ‖   :‖ *play 4 times*

	B **E5**
Pre-Chorus	I can't control it, can't even hold it.

B   **E5**
I can't control it, can't even hold it.

B   **E5**
It's sneaking up on your front door,

      B
You can feel it on your ankle.

E5
Feel it on your knee,

B   **E5**
Feel it on your thigh, can you feel me?

G D A   E
Put it right on you.

G D A   E
Put it right on you.

G D   A   E
   I'll do it if you want me to.

G D   G D G D
  Can I put it,

G   D   A E A E
  Can I put it?

	A E A E A5 G5/A
Chorus 3	I put the finger on you.

A E   A E   A5 G5/A
I put the finger on you.

D   **A5 G5/A**
|: I put the finger on you.   :| *play 7 times*

| **A5** | **D** | | **A5** | **D5** |

	So close,
Outro	**A5 D**

So close,

A5 D
  I hit the spot.

A5 D   **A5   E5**
  I put the finger right on you.

The Razors Edge

Words & Music by
Angus Young and Malcolm Young

freely

Intro
| (E) | | |
|: **E5** | | :| *play 8 times*
B5	**C5** **G5**
A5	**B5**
: **E5**		:

Verse 1

       E5
There's fighting on the left,

And marching on the right,

Don't look up in the sky,

You're gonna die of fright.

Chorus 1

B5 **C5**   **G5** **A5**   **B5**
Here comes the razor's edge.

Link

| **E5** | | |

Verse 2

       E5
You're living on the edge,

Don't know wrong from right.

They're breathing down your neck,

You're running out of lives,

	B5 C5 G5 A5 B5
Chorus 2	And here comes the razor's edge.
	C5 G5 A5 B5
	Here comes the razor's edge.

The razor's edge.

Interlude	‖: **E5**	:‖

	A5 G5 B5
Bridge	Razor's edge, to raise the dead.
	A5 G5 B5
	Razor's edge, to cut to shreds.

‖: **D5** | **G5**   :‖

To raise the dead.

Solo		**A5 G5	B5 |**
		**A5 G5	B5 |**
	‖: **E5	:‖**

| | **B5 C5   G5 A5   B5**
| **Chorus 3** | Here comes the razor's edge.
| | **   C5   G5 A5   B5**
| | Here comes the razor's edge.
| | **   C5**
| | Well, here it comes,
| | **G5   A5**
| | To cut to shreds.
| | **   B5**
| | The razor's edge.
| | **   E5**
| | It's the razor's edge.

Outro   By the razor's edge.

          That you'll be cut to shreds,

          That you'll be cut to shreds.

          Gotta razor's edge, by the razor's edge.

          | **E5** | | | | ‖

Ride On

Words & Music by
Angus Young, Malcolm Young and Bon Scott

Intro ‖: **C** **F** | **C** **F**   :‖

Verse 1

    C   **F** **C**
It's another lonely evening,
F   **B♭** **F**
 In another lonely town.
B♭ **G**   **C**
 But I ain't too young to worry,
   B♭   **F**
And I ain't too old to cry,
    C   **F** **C**
When a woman gets me down.
F   **C**   **F** **C**
 Got another empty bottle,
F   **B♭** **F**
 And another empty bed.
B♭ **G**   **C**
 Ain't too young to admit it,
   B♭   **F**
And I'm not too old to lie,
    C   **F** **C**
I'm just another empty head.
F   **F5**   **F♯5**
 That's why I'm lonely, I'm so lonely,
   G5
But I know what I'm gonna do.

| F   C   G |
| *Chorus 1* | I'm gonna ride on, ride on. |

Chorus 1

        F   C   G
I'm gonna ride on, ride on.
C   F
Ride on, standing on the edge of the road,
B♭ F
Ride on, thumb in the air.
F   C
Ride on, one of these days I'm gonna,
       G
Ride on, change my evil ways,
F
   Till then I'll just keep ridin' on.

Solo

‖: C   F | C   F   :‖

Verse 2

C   F   C
Broke another promise,
F   B♭ F
  And I broke another heart.
B♭   G   C
   But I ain't too young to realize,
       B♭   F
That I ain't too old to try,
     C   F C
Try to get back to the start.
C   F   C
  And it's another red light nightmare.
F   B♭ F
  Another red light street.
B♭   G   C
  And I ain't too old to hurry,
      B♭   F
'Cause I ain't too old to die.
     C   F   C
But I sure am hard to beat.
F   F5   F♯5
  But I'm lonely, Lord I'm lonely
G
  What am I gonna do?

F C G

Chorus 2   Ride on, ride on, got myself a one-way ticket,

F C B♭ F

Ride on, ride on, going the wrong way.

F C

Ride on, gonna change my evil ways,

      G

Ride on, one of these days,

F

   One of these days.

Solo   ‖: **C F** | **C F**   :‖
          | **F B♭** | **F B♭**
         ‖: **C   F** | **C F**   :‖ *play 3 times*
          | **F B♭** | **F B♭**
          | **C F** | **C F**
          | **F5** | **F♯5**
          | **G5**

F C   G

Chorus 3   Ride on, ride on,

                F C

I'm gonna ride on,

B♭ F

Ride on, looking for a truck,

F C   G

Ride on, ride on, keep on riding,

F5

   Riding on and on and on.

F C   G

Ride on, ride on, get myself a good time,

C F B♭ F

Ride on, ride on,

F C   **G**

Ride on, one of these days, ride on,

One of these days.

    | **F5** | **C**   ‖

Riff Raff

Words & Music by
Angus Young, Malcolm Young and Bon Scott

Intro

```
‖: D Dsus4 D Dsus4 | D Dsus4       |
 | D Dsus4 D Dsus4 | D/A      A :‖
‖: D Dsus4 D Dsus4 | D Dsus4       |
 | D Dsus4 D Dsus4 | D/A A      :‖  play 3 times
 | A               |          A5  |
‖: (A)      | A5    :‖  play 8 times
 | D   Dsus4 D |   | D Dsus4  D |
 | Dsus4 D Dsus4 A5 |
‖: (A)    | A5    :‖
 | D   Dsus4 D |   | D Dsus4  D |
 | Dsus4 D Dsus4 E7 |          |
 |              |          A5  |
‖: (A)    | A5    :‖  play 4 times
‖: A5     |       :‖
```

Verse 1

G5/A A5
　　See it on the television every day,
G5/A A5
　　Hear it on the radio,
G5/A A5
　　　It ain't humid but it sure is hot,
G5/A A5
　　Down in Mexico.
G5/A A5
　The boy is trying to tell me,
G5/A A5
　　Near enough to the edge,
G5/A A5
　Say they've all been there,
G5/A A5
　　Too late my friend.

Chorus 1

D   Dsus4 D
Riff raff,
Dsus4 D   Dsus4   D A5
Always good for a laugh.

‖: **(A)** | **A5**   :‖

D   Dsus4 D
Riff raff,
Dsus4 D   Dsus4   D   E7
Go on, laugh yourself in half.

Solo

‖: **A5** | :‖ *play 3 times*
| **A D   A** | **D A D5** |
‖: **D5** | :‖
| **A5** |
| **A D   A** | **D A E7** |
‖: **E7** | :‖ *play 4 times*
‖: **A5** | :‖ *play 3 times*
| **A D   A** | **D A D5** |
‖: **D5** | :‖
| **A5** |
| **A D   A** | **D A E7** |
‖: **E7** | :‖ *play 4 times*
‖: **A5** | :‖ *play 3 times*
‖: **(A)** | :‖
‖: **A5** | :‖ *play 6 times*

Verse 2

G5/A A5
Now I'm   the kind of guy,

Who keeps his big mouth shut.
G5/A A5
        It don't bother me,
G5/A A5
            Somebody kicking me when I'm up,
G5/A A5
        Living in misery.
G5/A A5
        I've never shot nobody,
G5/A A5
        Don't even carry a gun,
G5/A A5
            I ain't done nothing wrong,
G5/A A5
        I'm just having fun.

D   Dsus4 D
Chorus 2   Riff raff,

Dsus4 D   Dsus4   D A5
        Always good for a laugh.

‖: **(A)** | **A5**   :‖

D   Dsus4 D
Riff raff,
Dsus4 D   Dsus4   D   E7
        Go on, laugh yourself in half.

Outro   ‖: **(A)** | **A5**   :‖ *play 3 times*
        | **A5**   ‖

Rock And Roll
Ain't Noise Pollution

Words & Music by
Angus Young and Malcolm Young and Brian Johnson

Intro

| E |: A | | E5 | A E | :| *play 3 times*
| A | | E | A E | | E5
|: A G5 | E | A G5 E5 | :|

Verse 1

  E5   A
Heavy decibels are playin' on my guitar.
       E   A
We got vibrations comin' up from the floor.
           E
We're just listening to the rock,
             A
That's giving too much noise.
         E   A
Are you deaf, you wanna hear some more?
         E5   D5
We're just talkin' about the future,
B   E5
Forget about the past.
        D5
It'll always be with us,
A5
It's never gonna die, never gonna die.

Chorus 1

E   A   G5 E5
Rock 'n' roll ain't noise pollu – tion.
           A   G5 E5
Rock 'n' roll ain't gonna   die.
          A   G5 E5
Rock 'n' roll ain't no pollu – tion.
        A   G5 E5
Rock 'n' roll it will sur - vive.

Verse 2

    E5   **A**
I took a look inside your bedroom door,
    E5   **A**
You looked so good lying on your bed.
    E5
Well, I asked you if you wanted,
 A
Any rhythm and love,
       E5   **A**
You said you wanna rock 'n' roll instead.
       E5   **D5**
We're just talkin' about the future,
B   **E5**
Forget about the past.
      D5
It'll always be with us,
A5
It's never gonna die, never gonna die.

Chorus 2

E   **A**   **G5 E5**
Rock 'n' roll ain't noise pollu - tion.
       A   **G5 E5**
Rock 'n' roll ain't gonna die.
     A   **G5 E5**
Rock 'n' roll ain't no pollu – tion.
     A   **G5**   **E5**
Rock 'n' roll is just rock 'n' roll.

Solo

```
‖: E5      | A5    | E5   | A5    :‖
 | E5   D5 | B  E5 | E5 D5| A5    |
```

    E   **A**   **G5 E5**
Rock 'n' roll ain't noise pollu - tion.
           A   **G5 E5**
Rock 'n' roll ain't gonna   die.
           A   **G5 E5**
Rock 'n' roll ain't no pollu - tion.
      A   **G5 E5**
Rock 'n' roll it will sur - vive.
E   **A**   **G5 E5**
Rock 'n' roll ain't noise pollu - tion.
           A   **G5 E5**
Rock 'n' roll ain't gonna   die.
           A   **G5 E5**
Rock 'n' roll ain't no pollu - tion.
        D5 A5
Rock 'n' roll
          G5
Rock 'n' roll,
             E5
Is just rock 'n' roll.

Rock 'N' Roll Damnation

Words & Music by
Angus Young, Malcolm Young and Bon Scott

Intro

```
‖:A7          |          |
| D/A         |          :|
‖: A D/A   A  | D/A A A  :‖
```

Verse 1

```
              D/A        A    D/A
They say that you play too loud,
         A           D/A A D/A A
Well, baby that's tough.
              D/A        A      D/A
They say that you get too much,
         A         D/A A D/A A
Can't get enough.
                 D/A         A    D/A
They tell you that you look a fool,
         A        D/A     A    D/A
  And baby I'm a fool    for you.
         A         D/A        A        D/A
  They say that your mind's   diseased,
         A                D/A A D/A A
    Shake your stuff.
```

Chorus 1

```
              G       D      A    D/A A
And it's a rock 'n' roll damnation.
    G         D        A    D/A
Ma's own whippin' boy.
    G       D        A    D/A A
Rock 'n' roll damnation.
    D               E
Take a chance   while you still got the choice.
```

Link

```
‖: A  D/A   A  | D/A A  :‖
```

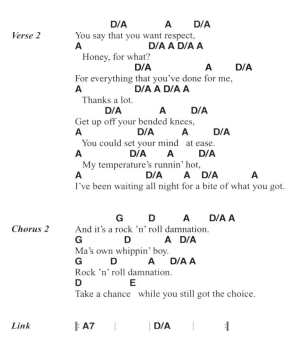

Verse 2

     D/A   **A** **D/A**
You say that you want respect,
A   **D/A A D/A A**
 Honey, for what?
     D/A   **A** **D/A**
For everything that you've done for me,
A   **D/A A D/A A**
 Thanks a lot.
   D/A **A** **D/A**
Get up off your bended knees,
A   **D/A** **A** **D/A**
 You could set your mind at ease.
A   **D/A** **A** **D/A**
 My temperature's runnin' hot,
A   **D/A** **A** **D/A**   **A**
I've been waiting all night for a bite of what you got.

Chorus 2

    G   **D**   **A** **D/A A**
And it's a rock 'n' roll damnation.
G   **D**   **A** **D/A**
Ma's own whippin' boy.
G   **D**   **A** **D/A A**
Rock 'n' roll damnation.
D   **E**
Take a chance while you still got the choice.

Link   ‖: **A7** | |**D/A** | :‖

	A7 **D/A**

Bridge
       A7   **D/A**
Damnation, they're puttin' you down.
       A7   **D/A**
Damnation, all over town.
       A7   **D/A**
Damnation, 'cause you're way outta reach,
A7
Livin' on the street,
       D/A
You gotta practice what you preach.

Chorus 3
           G   **D**   **A**   **D/A A**
And it's a rock 'n' roll damnation.
G   **D**   **A** **D/A**
Ma's own whippin' boy.
G   **D**   **A**   **D/A A**
Rock 'n' roll damnation.
G   **D**
Take a chance   while you still got the choice.

Link
‖: **A D/A** **A** | **D/A A** :‖

Outro
       D/A **A**   **D/A A**
Damnation, you left a happy home.
       D/A **A** **D/A**   **A**
Damnation,   to live on your own.
       D/A   **A**   **D/A A**
Damnation, you want to live in sin.
       D/A **A**   **D/A**   **A**
Damnation,   it's a rock 'n' roll.
       D/A A   **D/A**   **A**
Damnation,   just a bundle of joy,
       D/A **A**   **D/A**   **A**
Damnation, you're a toy for a boy.
       D/A **A**   **D/A**   **A**
Damnation, you got dollars in your eyes.
       D/A **A**   **D/A**   **A**
Damnation, always chasin' that pie in the sky.
       D/A A D/A   **A**
Damnation,   rock 'n' roll,
       D/A A D/A A
Damnation.

Rock 'N' Roll Singer

Words & Music by
Angus Young, Malcolm Young and Bon Scott

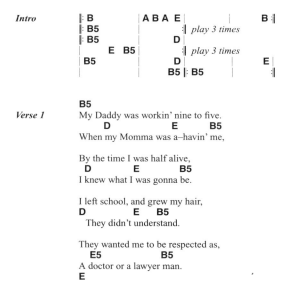

Intro

‖: **B** | **A B A E** | | **B** :‖
‖: **B5** | :‖ *play 3 times*
‖: **B5** | **D** :‖
| **E** **B5** | :‖ *play 3 times*
| **B5** | **D** | **E** |
| | **B5** ‖: **B5** | :‖

Verse 1

B5
My Daddy was workin' nine to five.
　　　D　　　　　**E**　　**B5**
When my Momma was a–havin' me,

By the time I was half alive,
　D　　　**E**　　　**B5**
I knew what I was gonna be.

I left school, and grew my hair,
D　　　**E**　**B5**
　They didn't understand.

They wanted me to be respected as,
　E5　　　　**B5**
A doctor or a lawyer man.
E
But I had other plans.

	B5 A5 E5 D5
Chorus 1	Gonna be a rock 'n' roll singer,

B5   A5 E5   D5
Chorus 1   Gonna be a rock 'n' roll singer,
B5   A5 E5   D5
   Gonna be a rock 'n' roll star.
B5   A5 E5   D5
   Gonna be a rock 'n' roll singer,
B5   A5 E
   I'm gonna be a rock 'n' roll,
           B5
A rock 'n' roll star.

Link   ‖: B5 | :‖

          B5
Verse 2   Well I worked real hard and bought myself,
          D   E   B5
A rock 'n' roll guitar.

I gotta be on top some day,
D   E   B5
   I wanna be a star.

I can see my name in lights,
D   E   B5
   And I can see the cue.

I got the devil in my blood,
E   B5
Tellin' me what to do.
E5
   And I'm all ears.

Chorus 2

B5   **A5** **E5**   **D5**
   Gonna be a rock 'n' roll singer,
B5   **A5** **E5**   **D5**
   Gonna be a rock 'n' roll star.
B5   **A5** **E5**   **D5**
   Gonna be a rock 'n' roll singer,
B5   **A5** **E**
   I'm gonna be a rock 'n' roll,
       B5
A rock 'n' roll star.
E5
   I hear it pays well.

Solo

B5		**D**	**E** **B5**		*play 3 times*
B5		**D**		**E**	
		B5	**B5**		

Bridge

       F♯5
Well you can stick your nine to five livin',

And your collar and your tie,
N.C.
And stick your moral standards,

'Cause it's all a dirty lie.
      F♯5
You can stick your golden handshake,

And you can stick your silly rules.

And all the other shit,
     E5   **B5**
That you teach the kids in school.
E5
   'Cause I ain't no fool.

| | **B5**   **A5 E5**   **D5**
Chorus 3 | Gonna be a rock 'n' roll singer,
| | **B5**   **A5 E5**   **D5**
| | Gonna be a rock 'n' roll star.
| | **B5**   **A5 E5**   **D5**
| | Gonna be a rock 'n' roll singer,
| | **B5**   **A5 E**
| | I'm gonna be a rock 'n' roll,

A rock 'n' roll star.
B5   **A5 E5**   **D5**
Gonna be a rock 'n' roll singer,
B5   **A5 E5**   **D5**
Gonna be a rock 'n' roll star.
B5   **A5 E5**   **D5**
Gonna be a rock 'n' roll singer,
B5   **A5 E**
I'm gonna be a rock 'n' roll,
                B5
A rock 'n' roll star.

Outro | **B5 A5 B5 A5 E** | |

Yes, I Are!

| **B5 A5 B5 A5 E** | ‖

208

Rocker

Words & Music by
Angus Young, Malcolm Young and Bon Scott

Tune down ½ step:
6 = E♭   3 = G♭
5 = A♭   2 = B♭
4 = D♭   1 = E♭

Intro

A					
D		**A**			
E		**A**			

Chorus 1   I'm a rocker, I'm a roller,

I'm a right out of controller.
D
I'm a wheeler, I'm a dealer,
   A
I'm a wicked woman stealer.
   E
I'm a bruiser, I'm a cruiser,
   A
A rockin' rollin' man.

A5
Verse 1   I got slicked back hair, skin tight jeans,

Cadillac car, and a teenage dream.

D
Chorus 2   I'm a rocker, I'm a roller,
   A
I'm a rocker, I'm a roller,
   E
I'm a rocker, I'm a roller,
   A
I'm a rockin' rollin' man.

Solo	‖: **A**				
	D		**A**		
	E		**A**		:‖

A5

Verse   I got lurex socks, blue suede shoes,

V8 car, and tattoos.

          D

Chorus 3   I'm a rocker, I'm a roller,
          A
I'm a rocker, I'm a roller,
          E
I'm a rocker, I'm a roller,
          A
I'm a rockin' rollin' man.

Solo	**A**				
	D		**A**		
	E		**A**		

	A
Chorus 4	I'm a rocker, I'm a roller,

I'm a rocker, I'm a roller,
D
I'm a rocker, I'm a roller,
A
I'm a rocker, I'm a roller,
E
I'm a rocker, I'm a roller,
A
I'm a rockin' rollin' man.
A
I'm a rocker, I'm a roller,

I'm a rocker, I'm a roller,
D
I'm a rocker, I'm a roller,
A
I'm a rocker, I'm a roller,
E
I'm a rocker, I'm a roller,
A
I'm a rock 'n' rollin' rock 'n' rollin' man.

Outro ‖: **A** | | | :‖ *repeat ad lib. to fade*

Safe In New York City

Words & Music by
Angus Young and Malcolm Young

freely

Intro

| **G5 A5** | **G5 A** | **G5 E5** | |
‖: **G5 A5 B♭5 A5** | **G5 A5 G5 E5** :‖ *play 5 times*
| **G5 A5 B♭5 A5** |

Verse 1

G5 A E
　　　Hello baby, give me your hand.
(E) E
　　　Check out the high spots, the lay of the land.
(E) E
　　　You don't need a rocket or a big limousine.
(E) E
　　　Ooh, come on over baby,

And I'll make you obscene.

Chorus 1

E5
I feel safe in New York City.

I feel safe in New York City.
G5 A5　B♭5 A5 G5　A5　G5 E5
I　　feel safe　in　New York Ci - ty.
G5 A5　B♭5　A5 G5　A5　G5 E5
I　　feel safe　in　New York Ci - ty.
| **G5 A5 B♭5 A5** |

Verse 2

G5 A E
　　　All over the city and all of the dives.
(E) E
　　　Don't mess with this place, it'll eat you alive.
(E) E
　　　Get a lip smackin' honey to soak off the jam.
(E) E
　　　On top of the world Ma, ready to slam.

Chorus 2

E5
I feel safe in New York City.

I feel safe in New York City.
G5 A5 B♭5 A5 G5   A5   G5 E5
I   feel safe   in   New York Ci - ty.
G5 A5 B♭5 A5 G5   A5   G5 E5
I   feel safe   in   New York Ci - ty.
G5 A5 B♭5 A5 G5   A5   G5 E5
I   feel safe   in   New York Ci - ty.
G5 A5 B♭5 A5 G5   A5   G5 A5
I   feel safe   in   New York Ci - ty.

Solo

‖: **C5 D5 E♭5 D5** | **C5 D5 C5 A5** :‖
| **C5 D5 E♭5 D5** | **E♭5 D5 E♭5 D5** | **E♭5 D5** |
‖: **G5 A5 B♭5 A5** | **G5 A5 G5 E5** |
| **G5 A5 B♭5 A5** | **(E)**   :‖

Verse 3

E5
Runnin' all over like a jumpin' bean,
(E) E
  Take a look at that thing in the tight assed jeans.
(E) E
   Comin' your way, now, you might be in luck,
(E) E
  Don't you fret boy, she's ready to buck.

Chorus 3

E5
I feel safe in New York City.

I feel safe in New York City.
G5 A5 B♭5 A5 G5 A5 G5 E5
I   feel safe in   New York Ci – ty.
G5 A5 B♭5 A5 G5 A5 G5 A5
I   feel safe in   New York Ci – ty.

Solo

‖: **C5 D5 E♭5 D5** | **C5 D5 C5 A5** :‖ *play 3 times*
| **C5 D5 E♭5 D5** | **E♭5 D5 E♭5 D5** | **E♭5 D5** |

Outro

E♭5 D5 B♭5 A5 G5 A5 G5 E5
I   feel safe in   New York Ci - ty.
   G5 A5 B♭5 A5 G5 A5 G5 E5
‖:I feel safe in   New York Ci - ty.
G5 A5 B♭5 A5 G5 A5 G5 E5
I   feel safe in   New York Ci - ty. :‖ *play 3 times*
G5   A5 B♭5 A5 G5 A
When it's rainin',
E5   G A5 E5   G5 A E5
New York,   New York,   New York,
G5 A5 E5
        I feel safe in a cage in New York City.
G5   A E
Throw away the key.

Satellite Blues

Words & Music by
Angus Young and Malcolm Young

Intro

‖: **G5/A A G5/A A** | **D** |
| **G5/D   D G5/D D** | :‖

Verse 1

A
She makes the place a jumpin',
D
The way she move around.
A
She like a romp and rollin',
D
That when she get it out.
A
And when she start a rockin',
D
She bring me to the boil.
A
She like to give it out some.

| **D G5/D D G5/D** |

Chorus 1

D   **A**   **D/F♯ G5**
New satellite blues, new satellite blues.
                  D   **D/F♯ G5**
New satellite blues, new satellite blues.

Verse 2

    A
A picture clear for watchin',
D
The dish is running hot.
A
The box is set for pumpin',
D
She gonna take the lot.
A
The way she get the butt in,
D
She's gettin' set to ball.

I like to chew it up some.

Chorus 2

D   **A**   **D/F♯ G5**
New satellite blues, new satellite blues.
                D   **D/F♯ G5**
New satellite blues, new satellite blues.
G C   **G C**   **G A**   **D/F♯ G5**
  New   satellite blues, new satellite blues.
                A   **D/F♯ G5**
New satellite blues, new satellite blues.
G C   **G**   **C G**
  Can't get nothing on the dial,
C   **G**   **C**   **G**
The friggin' thing's gone wild.
C   **G**   **C**   **G**   **D**
All I get is the dumbed down news.

New satellite blues, yeah.

Solo

```
‖: A        |   | D/F♯ G5 |           |
   A        |   | D/F♯ G5 | G C G C G |
   A        |   | D       |           |
   A        |   | D       |           |
   D        |
```

Chorus 3

> D   A   D/F♯ G5
> New satellite blues, new satellite blues.
> G   C   G C G A   D/F♯ G5
> Yeah, new satellite blues, new satellite blues.
> G C   G C   G A   D/F♯ G5
>   I got the satellite blues, new satellite blues.
> G C   G C G A   D/F♯ G5
>   New satellite blues, new satellite blues.
> G   C   G   C   G
> This thing's nothing but a load of crap,
> G C   G   C G
>   I'm gonna send it right back.
> G C   G   C G   D
>   You can stick it where it hurts, Mac.

Outro

> | G D G | D |

> Oh yeah, I got the new satellite blues.

> | A | ‖

Shake A Leg

Words & Music by
Angus Young and Malcolm Young and Brian Johnson

Intro   E5 | | A5 | E5 | :|

Verse 1
E5   **A5 E5**
Idle juvenile on the street, on the street.

Who is kicking everything,
                              A5 E5 A5 E5
With his feet, with his feet.

Fighting on the wrong side of the law,
                    A5 E5 A5 E5
Of the law.

Don't kick, don't fight, don't sleep at night,

And shake a leg, shake a leg,

Shake a leg, shake it yeah.

‖: **E5** | :‖

E5
Keeping out of trouble,

With eyes in the back of my face.

Kicking ass in the class,

And they tell me you're a damn disgrace.
        A5
They tell me what they think,

But they stink and I really don't care.
        E5
Got a mind of my own, move on, get out of my hair.

Chorus 1

   E/B B E/B   B
Ah, shake a leg, shake your head,
E/B B E/B   B
Shake a leg, wake the dead,
E/B B E/B   B
Shake a leg, get stuck in,
E/B B E/B B
Shake a leg,
B E/B B E/B
 Shake a leg.
   B
Yeow!

Link

 ‖: E5 | :‖

Verse 2

E5
Magazines, wet dreams,

Dirty women on machines for me.

Big licks, skin flicks, tricky dicks are my chemistry.
   A5
Goin' against the grain,

Trying to keep me sane, with you.
  E5
So stop your grinnin' and drop your linen for me.

Chorus 2

   E/B B E/B   B
Ah, shake a leg, shake your head,
E/B B E/B   B
Shake a leg, wake the dead,
E/B B E/B   B
Shake a leg, get stuck in,
E/B B E/B B
Shake a leg,
B E/B B E/B
 Shake a leg.
E5
Yeah, shake it!

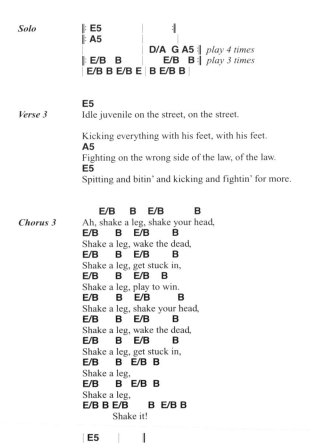

Solo

```
‖: E5         |         :‖
‖: A5         |            |
   |              | D/A  G A5 :‖  play 4 times
‖: E/B  B    |     E/B  B :‖  play 3 times
   | E/B B E/B E | B E/B B |
```

Verse 3

E5
Idle juvenile on the street, on the street.

Kicking everything with his feet, with his feet.
A5
Fighting on the wrong side of the law, of the law.
E5
Spitting and bitin' and kicking and fightin' for more.

Chorus 3

        E/B   B   E/B   B
Ah, shake a leg, shake your head,
E/B   B   E/B   B
Shake a leg, wake the dead,
E/B   B   E/B   B
Shake a leg, get stuck in,
E/B   B   E/B   B
Shake a leg, play to win.
E/B   B   E/B   B
Shake a leg, shake your head,
E/B   B   E/B   B
Shake a leg, wake the dead,
E/B   B   E/B   B
Shake a leg, get stuck in,
E/B   B E/B B
Shake a leg,
E/B   B E/B B
Shake a leg,
E/B B E/B   B E/B B
        Shake it!

| E5 | ‖
```
```

Shake Your Foundations

Words & Music by
Angus Young and Malcolm Young and Brian Johnson

Intro
| G5 | ‖: D5 | G7 |
| G5 G7 | G5 :‖

Verse 1

           D5   **G7**
You gotta   see me leanin' on the bar,
            G5   **G7**   **G5**
I got my head in a whiskey jar.
D5
   Feelin' good 'cos the city's alive,
G7   **G5** **G7**   **G5**
   I'm gettin' ready to rock and jive.
D5
   I get up and I slide across the floor,
G7   **G5**   **G7**   **G5**
   You wanna come and I'll meet you at the door.
D5   **G7**
   No one can stop us 'cos we're feelin' too right,
            G5 **G7**   **G5**
We're gonna steal our way around tonight.
G7 **G5** **G7** **G5**
   Alright,   alright.

Chorus

D5   **G5**
Aye, aye, oh, shake your foundations.
D5   **G5 G7**   **G5**
Aye, aye, oh, shake it to the floor.
D5   **G5**
Aye, aye, oh, shake your foundations,
D5   **G5 G7**   **G5**
Aye, aye, oh, shake it.

Link
| ‖: D5 | | G5 G7 | G5 :‖

Verse 2

G5   D5   G7
I was takin' no liberties,
             G5   G7
She's gettin' hotter off the heat on me.
G5   D5
I was oilin', she was slick,
G7   G5   G7   G5
Lickin' off the sweat, on her favorite trick.
          D5   G7
Yeah, help me, help me, please, yeah,
             G5   G7   G5
Tame this animal,   help me to breathe.
          D5   G7
I said, "No, no way,"
             G5   G7   G5 G7
You gotta come with me all of the way.
       G5 G7   G5
O.K.   I'll play.

Chorus 2

D5   G5
Aye, aye, oh, shake your foundations.
D5   G5 G7   G5
Aye, aye, oh, shake it to the floor.
D5   G5
Aye, aye, oh, shake your foundations,
D5   G5 G7   G5
Aye, aye, oh,   shake it to the floor.

Solo

A5	D5 A5		D5 C	G5	
C5	G5		D5 A5	D5 C5
	G5	C5	G5 A5	G5	

Chorus 3

D5   G5
Aye, aye, oh, shake your foundations.
D5   G5 G7   G5
Aye, aye, oh,   shake it to the floor.
D5   G5
Aye, aye, oh, shake your foundations,
D5   G5 G7   G5
Aye, aye, oh,   shake it.

Verse 3

D5   G7
We had the night, we had the time.
              G5 G7   G5
She had the sugar, and I had the wine.
D5   G7
   Took my hand, shook me to the core.

Told her not to touch,
G5   G7   G5
   But she was coming back for more.
   G5 G7   G5
You know   what for.

Chorus 4

D5   G5
Aye, aye, oh, shake your foundations.
D5   G5 G7   G5
Aye, aye, oh, shake it to the floor.
D5   G5
Aye, aye, oh, shake your foundations,
D5   G5 G7   G5
Aye, aye, oh, shake it to the floor.
D5   G5
Aye, aye, oh, shake your foundations.
D5   G5 G7   G5
Aye, aye, oh, shake it to the floor.
D5   G5
Aye, aye, oh, shake your foundations,
D5 G5   D5
     Make you so eager.

She's Got Balls

Words & Music by
Angus Young, Malcolm Young and Bon Scott

Intro

```
‖: Am7          |        :‖ play 3 times
‖: D5/A Am7     |                        :‖
  D5/A  Am7   | F5   |              |   G |
             | C   | Am7  |
  D5/A Am7   |
```

Verse 1

She's got style, that woman,
       D5/A Am7
Makes me smile,   that woman,

She's got spunk, that woman,
    D5/A Am7
Funk, that   woman.

She's got speed, my baby,
       D/A Am7
Got what I need, my baby,

She's got the ability,
       D5/A Am7
To make a man outta me.

        G

Chorus 1   But most important of all,

Let me tell you,
C   **A5**
Ow! The lady's got balls.
C5   **A5**
She's got balls.
C5   **A5**
She's got balls.
C5   **A5 C5**
She's got balls.

Verse 2

Am7
She's got soul, my lady,
         D5/A Am7
Likes to crawl,   my lady,

All around the floor,
       D5/A Am7
On her hands and   knees,
          D5/A Am7
Oh, because she likes to please me.

                   G
Chorus 2   But most important of all,

Let me tell you,
C   **A5**
Ow! The lady's got balls.
C5   **A5**
She's got balls.
C5   **A5**
She's got balls.
C5   **A5 C5**
She's got balls.

Solo | **Am7** | | **D5/A Am7** |
         | **D5/A Am7** | **C5 D5** | **Am7** |

Verse 3	**Am7**
	And she's got taste my lady,
	D5/A Am7 **D5/A**
	Pace my lady,
	Am7
	Makes my heart race,
	D5/A Am7
	With her pretty face.
	D5/A Am7
	She's got balls, my lady,
	D5/A
	Likes to crawl, my lady,
	Am7
	Hands and knees, all around the floor,
	Am7
	No-one has to tell her, what a fella is for.
	F **G**
Chorus 3	But let me tell you all,
	C **A5**
	Mmm, yeah, the lady's got balls.
	C5 **A5**
	She's got balls.
	C5 **A5**
	She's got balls.
	C5 **A5**
	She's got balls.
	C5 **A5**
	She's got balls.
	C5 **A5**
	My lady's got balls.
	C5
	Takin' it out!
Outro	| **F5** | **G** | — |
	C **A5**
	She's got balls.

Shoot To Thrill

Words & Music by
Angus Young and Malcolm Young and Brian Johnson

Intro

A5					
‖: **G5 D G5**	**D A5**		:‖	*play 8 times*	

Verse 1

                        G5   **D**   **G5**   **D**
All you women   who want a man of the street,
A5   **G5**   **D**   **G5 D**
    But don't know which way you wanna turn.
A5   **G5**   **D**   **G5**   **D**
    Just keep a–coming   and put your hand out to me,
A5   **G5**   **D**   **G5**
'Cause I'm the one who's gonna make you burn.
        C G   **C**   **G**   **C**
I'm gonna take you down, ah, down, down, down.
        D   **A**   **D**
So don't you fool around.
                    E7♯9
I'm gonna   pull it, pull it, pull the trigger.

Chorus 1

A5   **G5**
Shoot to thrill,   play to kill,
D/A
        Too many women with too many pills, yeah.
A5   **G5**
Shoot to thrill,   play to kill,
            D/A
I got my gun at the ready, gonna fire at will, yeah!

A5					

Verse 2

            G5 D   G5   D
I'm like evil,   I get under your skin,
A5   G5 D   G5   D
   Just like a bomb that's ready to blow.
A5   G5 D G5   D
   'Cause I'm illegal,   I got everything,
       A5   G5   D   G5
That all you women might need to know.
    C G   C   G   C
I'm gonna take you down, ah, down, down, down.
    D   A   D
So don't you fool around.
         E7♯9
I'm gonna   pull it, pull it, pull the trigger.

Chorus 2

A5   G5
Shoot to thrill,   play to kill,
D/A
   Too many women with too many pills, yeah.
A5   G5
Shoot to thrill, play to kill,
   D/A
I got my gun at the ready, gonna fire at will, yeah!
A5   G
Shoot to thrill, and I'm ready to kill,
D/A
I can't get enough, and I can't get my fill.
   A5   G5
I shoot to thrill,   play to kill
D/A   E7♯9
   Yeah, pull the trigger.

Pull it, pull it, pull it, pull the trigger.

Solo

‖: **G5 D/A   G5** | **D/A**   :‖ *play 4 times*
| **C   G   C** | | **G   C** |
| **D   A   D** | **E7♯9** |

Chorus 3

A5   **G5**
Shoot to thrill,   play to kill,
D/A
    Too many women, with too many pills.
      A5   **G5**
I said, shoot to thrill,   play to kill,
     D/A
I got my gun at the ready, gonna fire at will.
       A5   **G5**
'Cause I shoot to thrill, and I'm ready to kill,
     D/A
And I can't get enough, and I can't get my thrill.
       A5   **G5**   **D/A**
'Cause I   shoot to thrill, play to kill.

‖: **A5** | **G** | **D** | :‖ *repeat ad lib. to end*

Shot Down In Flames

Words & Music by
Angus Young, Malcolm Young and Bon Scott

Intro

| D5 | | | **A** | |
|:‖ **A5 G5** | **D5 C5** :‖ *play 4 times* |

Verse 1

　　A5　　**G5**　　**D5**　　　**C5**
Out on the town, looking for a woman,
　　A5　　　　　　**D5 C5**
　　Gonna give me good love.
　　A5　**G5**　　　**D5**　　　　**C5**
　　Anybody want to hang out with me?
　　A5　　**G5**　　　**D5**
　　I'm really burnin' up.
C5　　　　　**A5**　**G5**　**D5**　　**C5**
　　She was standin' alone, over by the jukebox,
　A5　**G5**　　　　　　**D5 C5**
　　Like she's something to sell.
A5　　**G5**　　　　**D5 C5**
　　I said baby what's the going price?
　　　A5　**G5**　　**D5**
She told me to go to hell.

Chorus 1

　　　　　　　A5　**G5 D5**
Shot down in flames.
C5　　　　　**A5**　**G5 D5**
　　Shot down in flames.
C5　　**A5**　**G5 D5**
Ain't it a shame,
　　C5　　　　　**A5**　**G5 D5**
To be shot down in flames.

	A5	**G5**		**D5**	**C5**

Verse 2

       A5   **G5**   **D5**   **C5**
Singles bar, got my eye on a honey,
       A5   **G5**   **D5** **C5**
   Hanging out everywhere.
             A5   **G5**
She might be straight,
       D5   **C5**
She might want my money,
       A5   **G5**   **D5** **C5**
   I really don't care, no.
       A5   **G5**   **D5**   **C5**
   Said, baby, you're driving me crazy,
       A5   **G5**   **D5** **C5**
   Laid it out on the line.
       A5   **G5**   **D5**   **C5**
   When a guy with a chip on his shoulder said,
       A5   **G5**   **D5**
   "Don't sit, buddy, she's mine."

Chorus 2

                 A5   **G5 D5**
Shot down in flames.
       C5   **A5**   **G5 D5**
   Shot down in flames.
       C5   **A5**   **G5 D5**
Ain't it a shame,
        C5   **A5**   **G5 D5**
To be shot down in flames.

Solo

‖: **A5 G5** | **D5 C5** :‖ *play 7 times*
 | **A5 G5**   ‖: **D5** | :‖

	A5		**G5 D5**

Chorus 3

               A5   **G5 D5**
Shot down in flames.
C5   **A5**   **G5 D5**
  Shot down in flames.
C5   **A5**   **G5 D5**
Ain't it a shame,
   C5   **A5**   **G5 D5**
To be shot down in flames.
              A5   **G5 D5**
Shot down in flames.
C5   **A5**   **G5 D5**
  Shot down in flames.
C5   **A5**   **G5 D5**
Ain't it a shame,
   C5   **A5**   **G5**
To be shot down in flames.

D5

Outro

I, don't, don't leave me!
          A5
Shot down in flames.

Show Business

Words & Music by
Angus Young, Malcolm Young and Bon Scott

Intro

E5	A5	E5		
A5		E5		F♯5
A5		E5	B7 A5

E5

Verse 1 You learn to sing,

You learn to play.

Why don't the businessman,

Ever learn to pay?

A5

Chorus 1 Show business, show business,
E5
Show business, show business,
F♯5   **A5**
Show business,   that's the way it goes.
| E5 | | B7 A5 |

E5

Verse 2 You play in halls,

You play in bars.

You're climbin' walls,

Chasin' stars.

Chorus 2

A5
   Show business, show business,
E5
   Show business, show business,
F5   F♯5   G♯5 A5 A♯5   B5   E5 B7
Show business,   that's the way it goes.

Solo

E5	A5	E5	A5	
A5		E5		F♯5
A5		E5		B7
E5	A5	E5	A5	
A5		E5		F♯5
F5 F♯5 G♯5 A5	A♯5 B5 G5	E5		B7

Verse 3

E5
You pay the men,

You pay your dues.

When it's all gone,

You sing the blues.

Chorus 3

A5
   Show business, show business,
E5
   Show business, show business,
F♯5   A5
   Show business,   that's the way it goes.
| E5 | | B7 A5 |

E5

Verse 4   You wanna roll,

You wanna rock.

But you find it hard,

If your guitar's in hock.

A5

Chorus 4   Show business, show business,
E5
    Show business, show business,
F5   F♯5   G♯5 A5 A♯5   B5   E5 B7
Show business,   that's the way it goes.

Solo

E5		A5		E5		A5	
A5				E5			F♯5
		A5		E5			B7
E5		A5		E5		A5	
A5				E5			F♯5
F5 F♯5 G♯5 A5		A♯5 B5 G5	E5		B7

E5

Verse 5   We smoke our butts,

They smoke cigars.

We drown in debt,

They drown in bars.

Sin City

Words & Music by
Angus Young, Malcolm Young and Bon Scott

Intro

```
    |(E)          |           |           |
    |: E5  B5     | D5    A :| play 7 times
    | E   B       |: D        :|
```

Verse 1

```
E           B5 D5 A5    E5 B5 D5
Diamonds         and dust,
A5          E5 B5 D5 A5            E5 B5 D5
   Poor man last,         rich man first.
A5           E5 B5 D5 A5    E5 B5 D5
   Lambourginis,         caviar,
A5           B5 D5 A5      E5 B5 D5
   Dry martinis,        Shangri-la.
A5
   I got a burning feeling,

Deep inside of me,
     B
Lit the oven,

But I'm going to set it free.
```

Chorus 1

```
           E  B D A      E   B D
I'm going in       to sin city,
A       E   B D A       E   B D E
  I'm gonna win       in sin city,
B        D       A   E
Where the lights are bright,
B        D     A
Do the town tonight,
          E  B D A      E   B5
I'm gonna win       in sin city.

Hey, I'm gonna burn you, baby.
```

Copyright © 1978 by J. Albert & Son Pty., Ltd.
International Copyright Secured. All Rights Reserved.

Solo

```
|: E   B  | D   A   :| play 7 times
|  E5  B5 | D   |    |    |
|  (E)    |     |    |    |
|: E5  B5 | D5  A5 :|
```

Verse 2

E   BDA   E   BD
Ladders   and snakes,

A   E BDA   E BD
  Ladders give,   snakes take.

A   E BDA   E BD
  Rich man, poor man,   beggar man, thief,

A   B BD   E   BD
  Ain't got a hope in hell,   that's my belief.

A   EBDA   E BD
  Fingers Freddy,   Diamond Jim,

A   E BD
  They're getting ready,

A   E BDA
Look out I'm coming in.

E G A
   So spin that wheel, cut that pack,

   A
And roll those loaded dice,

B5
   Bring on the dancing girls,

And put the champagne on ice.

Chorus 2

```
                E  B D A     E  B D
I'm going in            to sin city,
A            E   B D A       E   B D E
 I'm gonna win        in sin city,
B        D        A    E
Where the lights are bright,
B        D        A
Do the town tonight,
               E  B D A        E   B5 D
I'm gonna win          in sin city.
```

| (E)   ‖

Sink The Pink

Words & Music by
Angus Young and Malcolm Young and Brian Johnson

Intro | N.C. | ‖: G5 | :‖ *play 5 times*
          ‖: Csus4 C | Csus4 C G5 :‖ *play 3 times*

                 Csus4 C   Csus4 C

Verse 1   Put your gear into   fire,
           Csus4   C   Csus4 C   Csus4 C
             Lay your bullets on the   ground.
           Csus4   C   G5 Csus4   C   Csus4 C
             Turn your head to   desire,
           Csus4   C G5   Csus4 C   Csus4 C
             There's a woman goin'   down.
           Csus4   G/B C5   G/B
             She says she'll rough you up,   all the way,
           C5   G/B C5   G/B C5   G/B
            Then she's gon–na spit you out,   count your days.
           C5   G/B D5   C5
            She says,   "Choice is yours,"   casually,
           D5   B♭5
           "So, why don't you do what comes naturally?"

             G5 Csus4 C

Chorus 1   Sink the pink,
           Csus4 C G5   Csus4 C
             It's all the fashion.
           Csus4 C G5   Csus4 C
             Drink the drink,
           Csus4 C G5   Csus4 C
             It's old-fashioned.
           Csus4 C G5   Csus4 C
             Gimme water,
             G5 Csus4 C
           Gimme wine.

```
              G5              Csus4 C
Gonna show you,
              G5
A good time.
Csus4 C          G5  Csus4 C
    Sink the pink,
Csus4 C  G5  Csus4 C
        Sink the pink.


              G5   Csus4 C   Csus4 C
Verse 2    Got a fever runnin' high,
           Csus4      C          Csus4   C Csus4 C
               Give you wings to make you fly.
           Csus4 C                 Csus4 C   Csus4 C
               She schooled you like a  fool,
           Csus4 C    G5        Csus4  C   Csus4 C
               She'll make you break the rules.
           Csus4      C        G/B C5    G/B
               She's gonna get a shot, hit that spot,
           C5        G/B C5        G/B C5   G/B
               Then I'm gon–na rack 'em up,  get it hot.
           C5    G/B D5           C5
               She said,   "Make it good,   satisfy."
           D5                       B♭5
               You know that woman got      jealous eyes.


              G5  Csus4 C
Chorus 2   Sink the pink,
           Csus4 C G5              Csus4 C
               It's all the fashion.
           Csus4 C G5           Csus4 C
               Drink the drink,
           Csus4 C G5             Csus4 C
               It's old-fashioned.
           Csus4 C G5          Csus4 C
               Gimme water,
              G5  Csus4 C
           Gimme wine.
              G5          Csus4 C
           Gonna show you,
```

        G5
A good time.
Csus4 C   **G5**   **Csus4 C**
     Sink the pink,
Csus4 C G5   **Csus4 C**
       Sink the pink.

Solo   ‖: **(G)** | :‖ **F5** | |
       | **G5** | | **C5** |
     ‖: **G/B** **C5** | **G/B C5 G/B C5** :‖ *play 3 times*
     | **G/B** **C5** | **G/B C5 G/B D5** | **C5** |
     | | **D5** | **B♭5** | |

        G5 Csus4 C
Chorus 3 Sink the pink,
      Csus4 C G5   **Csus4 C**
        It's all the fashion.
      Csus4 C G5   **Csus4 C**
        Drink the drink,
      Csus4 C G5   **Csus4 C**
        It's old-fashioned.
      Csus4 C G5   **Csus4 C**
        Gimme water,
        G5 Csus4 C
     Gimme wine.
        G5   **Csus4 C**
     Gonna show you,
        G5
     A good time.
      Csus4 C   **G5**   **Csus4 C**
       Sink the pink,
      Csus4 C G5   **Csus4 C**
        Sink the pink.
            G5
     Ow! Sink the pink!

Spellbound

Words & Music by
Angus Young and Malcolm Young and Brian Johnson

Intro ‖: **A5 C/A | G/A A5 | F/A | D/A** :‖ *play 4 times*

A5   **C/A G/A**

Verse 1 Blinded by a bright beam,
A5   **F/A D/A**
Shattered by the windscreen.
A5   **C/A G/A**
Stung by the whiplash,
   A5   **F/A D/A**
I'm the victim of a bad crash.

A5   **C/A G/A**

Pre-Chorus   I can't do nothing right,
A5   **C/A G/A**
  I never sleep at night.
A5   **C/A**
   Can't even start a fight,
G/A   D5
Oh, my feet have left the ground.

Spinning round and round.

A5   **G/B**   **C5**   **G/B**   **A5**

Chorus 1 Spellbound,   my world keeps a-tumbling down.
A5   **G/B**   **C5**   **G/B**   **A5**
Spellbound,   my world keeps a–tumbling down.

Verse 2

A5   C/A G/A
Leading by a blind man,
A5   F/A D/A
Wrong way up a dead end.
A5   C/A G/A
Screaming through a speed trap,
      A5   F/A D/A
As I tear into a tailback.

Pre-Chorus

A5   C/A   G/A
  I can't do nothing right,
A5   C/A G/A
  I never sleep at night.
A5   C/A
   Can't even start a fight,
G/A   D5
Oh, my feet have left the ground.

Spinning round and round.

Chorus 2

A5   G/B   C5   G/B   A5
Spellbound,   my world keeps a–tumbling down.
A5   G/B   C5   G/B   A5
Spellbound,   my world keeps a-tumbling down.
G5   E5
  It keeps a-tumbling down.

Solo

E5		A5	
C/A A5 G/A A5 D		C/A G/A A5
	C/A G/A D		C G/B
A5			

I got my hands in the fire.

	A5 **C/A G/A**

Verse 3
      A5   **C/A G/A**
I'm sliding on an oil slick,
      A5   **C/A**   **G/A**
Burnin' on a bad trip.
          A5   **C/A G/A**
Yes, and nothing's going to change it.

      D5

Pre-Chorus   No, I can't do nothing right,

Can't even sleep at night.

My feet have left the ground,

I'm spinning round and round.

      A5   **G/B**   **C5**   **G/B**   **A5**

Chorus 3   Spellbound,   my world keeps a-tumbling down.
      A5   **G/B**   **C5**   **G/B**   **A5**
Spellbound,   my world keeps a-tumbling down.
      A5   **G/B**   **C5**   **G/B**   **A5**
Spellbound,   my world keeps a-tumbling down.
      A5   **G/B**   **C5**   **G/B**   **A5**
Spellbound,   my world keeps a-tumbling down.

Squealer

Words & Music by
Angus Young, Malcolm Young and Bon Scott

Intro   ‖: **F**   **G5** | **D5** | | :‖ *play 4 times*
           ‖: **D5**   :‖ *play 5 times*

Verse 1
          D5
She said she'd never been,

Never been touched before.
     B5
She said she'd never been,
     D5
This far before.

She said she'd never liked,

To be excited.
         B
She said she'd always had,
  D5
Had to fight it, and she never won.
         C5 D5   **C5 D5**
She said she'd never been,
          C5 D5 **C5 D5**
Never been balled before.
B/A B5   **B/A B5**
   And I don't think,
        C5   **D5**
She'll ever ball no more,
      C5 D5
Fixed her good.

Chorus 1

        C5   **D5**
Hey! squealer, when I held her hand,
C5   **D5**
Squealer, made her understand.
C5   **D5**
Squealer, when I kissed her lips,
C5   **D5**
Squealer, and sucked her finger tips.
B/A **B5**
Squealer, she started getting hot,
B/A **B5**
Squealer, made it hard to stop.
C5   **D5**
Squealer, it got too much,
C5   **D5**
Squealer, I think I've got the magic touch.

Solo

‖: **B/A B5 B/A B5** | **B/A B5** |
B/A B5 B/A B5	**B/A B5**
C5 D5 **C5 D5**	**C5 D5**
C5 D5 **C5 D5**	**C5 D5** :
‖: **F5**   **G5**
C5 D5	:| *play 5 times*

‖: **C5 D5**   **C5 D5** | **C5 D5** |
  | **F5**   **G5** | :| *repeat to fade*

Stand Up

Words & Music by
Angus Young, Malcolm Young and Brian Johnson

Intro   ‖: **D5** | :‖

                     D5
Verse 1   Put on the headset, get on the stage.

             Out on a midnight escapade.
             G7
             Didn't want to steal your thunder,

             Wouldn't want to play your game.
                          D5
             Makin' all the headlines,

             Gettin' on the front page.

             G7
Pre-Chorus Ah, ah, didn't even know her number,

              I didn't even know her name.

             D5   **G5** **F5** **C/E**   **G5** **F5**
Chorus 1   Stand up, stand up and take it,
             D5   **G5** **F5** **C/E**   **G5** **F5**
             Stand up, stand up and make it,
             D5   **G5** **F5** **C/E**   **G5** **F5**
             Stand up, stand up and face it,
             D5   **G5**
             Stand up.

Verse 2

          D5
Get on the red dress, slip on the lace.

Up for a high heel and a pretty face.
G7
Woman wanna get you under,

Woman wanna get you tame.
         D5
Lovin' on a hot night,

Stokin' up the flame.

Pre-Chorus

G7
Ah, ah, didn't even know her number,

I didn't even know her name.

Chorus 2

D5   **G5 F5** **C/E**   **G5 F5**
Stand up, stand up and take it,
D5   **G5 F5** **C/E**   **G5** **F5**
Stand up, stand up and make it,
D5 **G5 F5** **C/E** **G5 F5**
Stand up, stand up and face it,
D5   **G5**
Stand up.
A5
   You can make it!

Solo   ‖: **A5** | :‖ *play 4 times*

G7

Pre-Chorus   Ah ah, didn't even know her number,

I didn't even know her name.

D5   G5 F5 C/E   G5 F5
Chorus 3   Stand up, stand up and take it,
D5   G5 F5   C/E   G5   F5
Stand up, stand up and make it,
D5   G5 F5   C/E   G5 F5
Stand up, stand up and face it,
D5   G5
Stand up.
F5 C/E G5
You can make it!
D5   C5 F5 C/E   G5 F5
Stand up, stand up and take it,
D5   C5 F5   C/E   G5   F5
Stand up, stand up and make it,
D5   C5 F5   C/E   G5 F5
Stand up, stand up and face it,
D5   G5 D5   G5
Stand up, stand up.

Outro | **F5 C/E G5** | | **D5** | ‖

249

Stiff Upper Lip

Words & Music by
Angus Young and Malcolm Young

Intro　　　　**A5** |:　　　　|　 **D C A5** :|

　　　　　　　　　　　　　　A5

Verse 1　　Well, I was out on a drive,
　　　　　　　　　　　　D　C A5
　　　　　　On a bit of a trip.

　　　　　　Lookin' for thrills,
　　　　　　　　　　D　　　　**C**
　　　　　　To get me some kicks.
　　　　　　　　A5
　　　　　　Now I warn you ladies,
　　　　　　　　D
　　　　　　I shoot from the hip.
　　　　　C　　　**A5**　　　　**N.C.**
　　　　　　I was born with a stiff,

　　　　　　Stiff upper lip.

　　　　　　　　　　　　A5　　　　　**D5**

Verse 2　　Like a dog in a howl,
　　　　　　C5 A5　　　　　　**D5**
　　　　　　　I bite everything.
　　　　　　C5　　　　**A5**　　　　　　**D5**
　　　　　　　And I'm big and I'm drawl,
　　　　　　C5　　　　**A5**　　　　　**D5**
　　　　　　　And I'll ball your thing.

	C5	A5	D5

Chorus 1

```
      C5              A5              D5
       And I  keep a stiff upper lip,
      C5      A5              D5
       And I shoot from the hip.
      C5      A5          D5
       I keep a stiff upper lip,
      C5          D5
       And I shoot,     and I shoot,
                        A5
      Shoot from the hip.
      D5   C5                          D5
      Yeah, shoot from the hip, now listen.
```

Verse 3

```
      C5          A5          D5
       Well I'm workin' it out,
      C5          A5          D5
       And I've done everything.
      C5      A5          D5
       And I can't reform, no;
      C5          A5          D5
       Can you feel my sting?
```

Chorus 2

```
      C5              A5              D5
       And I  keep a stiff upper lip,
      C5      A5              D5
       And I shoot from the hip.
      C5      A5          D5
       I keep a stiff upper lip,
      C5      D5
       And I shoot,    and I shoot,

      And I shoot, shoot, shoot,

      Yeah, shoot from the hip.
```

Solo	‖: **A5**		**D5**	**C5**	**A5** :‖	*play 3 times*
	A5		**D5**	**C5**		
	E					
	D5				**A5**	
	‖: **A5**		**D5**	**C5**	**A5** :‖	

Verse 4

        A5   **D5**
Well I'm out on the prowl, yeah,
C5   **A5**   **D5**
  And I'll ball your thing.
C5   **D5**
  I've got the teeth that'll bite you,
C5   **A5**   **D5**
  Can you feel that sting?

Chorus 3

C5   **A5**   **D5**
Babe, I keep a stiff upper lip,
C5   **A5**   **D5**
  And I shoot from the hip.
C5   **A5**   **D5**
  I keep a stiff upper lip,
C5   **N.C.**
  And I shoot, shoot, shoot from the hip.
     A5
I got a stiff upper lip,
D5   **C**   **A5**
  Better believe me, stiff upper lip.
D   **C**   **A5**   **D/A**
Comin' down, stiff upper lip.
C/A   **A5**
  See my, stiff upper lip.
D5 **C5**   **A5**   **D5 C5**
Yeah,   I got a stiff upper lip.

A5   **D5 C5**
   Stiff upper lip,
A5   **D5**
  Stiff upper lip.
C5 A5   **D5**
  I got a stiff upper lip.
C5 **A5**   **D5 C5**
I got a stiff upper lip.
A5   **D5**
Stiff upper lip,
C5 **A5**   **D5**
I got a stiff upper lip.
C5   **A5**
   And I shoot, and I shoot,

And I shoot, shoot from the hip.

T.N.T.

Words & Music by
Angus Young, Malcolm Young and Bon Scott

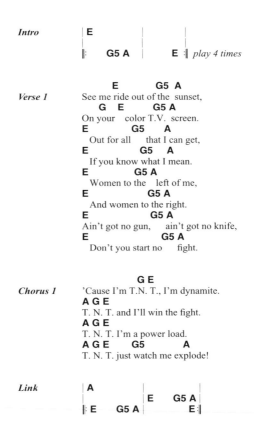

Intro

| E | |
| G5 A | E :|| *play 4 times*

Verse 1

           E   G5 A
See me ride out of the sunset,
        G   E   G5 A
On your   color T.V. screen.
E   G5   A
  Out for all   that I can get,
E   G5   A
  If you know what I mean.
E   G5 A
  Women to the left of me,
E   G5 A
  And women to the right.
E   G5 A
Ain't got no gun,   ain't got no knife,
E   G5 A
  Don't you start no   fight.

Chorus 1

               G E
'Cause I'm T.N. T., I'm dynamite.
A G E
T. N. T. and I'll win the fight.
A G E
T. N. T. I'm a power load.
A G E   G5   A
T. N. T. just watch me explode!

Link

A	
	E G5 A
	E G5 A	E :|

Verse 2

             G5   **A**
I'm dirty, mean, and mighty unclean.
G   E G5 A
I'm a wanted man,
E   **G5**   **A**
  Public enemy   number one,
E   G5 A
  Ya understand?
E
   So, lock up your daughter,
G5   **A**
   And lock up your wife,
E   **G5**   **A**
   Lock up your backdoor,   and run for your life.
E   **G5**   **A**
  The man is back in town,
E   **G5**   **A**
  So, don't you mess me 'round.

Chorus 2

            G E
'Cause I'm T.N. T., I'm dynamite.
A G E
T. N. T. and I'll win the fight.
A G E
T. N. T. I'm a power load.
A G E   **G5**   **A**
T. N. T. just watch me explode!

Solo

‖: **E**   **G A** | **G** **E** :‖ *play 3 times*
| **E**   **G A** |

Chorus 3

A G E
T. N. T. Oi! Oi! Oi!
A G E
T. N. T. Oi! Oi! Oi!
A G E
T. N. T. Oi! Oi! Oi!
A G E
T. N. T. Oi! Oi! Oi!

Chorus 4

    A G E
T. N. T., I'm dynamite.
    A G E
T. N. T. and I'll win the fight.
    A G E
T. N. T. I'm a power load.
    A G E   **G5**   **A**
T. N. T. just watch me explode!

Outro

E		**F**		**F♯**		**G**	
G♯	**A**	**A♯**	**B**	**C C♯ D D♯**	**E F F♯ G**
G♯5 A5 A♯5 B5			**E**		

That's The Way I Wanna Rock 'N' Roll

Words & Music by
Angus Young, Malcolm Young and Brian Johnson

Intro	‖: **A5**	**C5**	**A5**	**N.C.**	**A5** :‖ *play 3 times*
		A5	**C5**	**A5**	**N.C.**	**G5 D5**
		A5	**C5**	**A5**		

Verse 1

    A5   **C5**
Party gonna happen at the union hall,
    A5   **C5**
    Shaking to the rhythm 'til everybody fall.
    A5   **C5**
    Picking up my woman in my Chevrolet.
    A5   **D5**
    Glory hallelujah, gonna rock the night away.

Chorus 1

               A5
I'm gonna roll, roll, roll.
               G5
I'm gonna roll, roll, roll.
               D/F♯
I'm gonna take this town, turn it around.
               G5
I'm gonna roll, roll, roll.

Verse 2

    A5
Now there's a blue suede,
                              C5
Bopping on a high-heeled shoe,
    A5   **C5**
    Balling round together like a wrecking crew.
    A5   **C5**
    Oh, be bop a lula, baby what I say.
    A5
    You gotta get a dose of rock 'n' roll,
                           D5
On each and every day.

		A5
Chorus 2	I'm gonna roll, roll, roll.	

A5

Chorus 2   I'm gonna roll, roll, roll.

G5

I'm gonna roll, roll, roll.

D/F♯

I'm gonna take this town, turn it around.

G5

I'm gonna roll, roll, roll.

                    C5   **D5**

Bridge   I'm gonna   blow up my video,

C5   **D5**

   Shut down my radio.

                F5

I told boss man where to go.

D5   **F5**

   Turned off my brain control.

A5

That's the way I want my rock 'n' roll.

                       C5

That's the way I want my rock 'n' roll.

A5

   That's the way!

Solo | **A5** | | **C5** | **A5** |
	C5		
	A5	**C5**	**A5 C5**
	D5		

Interlude   That's the way I want my rock 'n' roll.

That's the way I want my rock 'n' roll.

That's the way, that's the way,

That's the way I want my rock 'n' roll.

That's the way, that's the way,

That's the way I want my rock 'n' roll.

That's the way, that's the way,

A5

Chorus 3   Oh, roll, roll, roll.
                    G5
I'm gonna roll, roll, roll.
                    D/F♯
I'm gonna take this town, turn it around.
                    G5
I'm gonna roll, roll, roll.
                    A5
I'm gonna roll, roll, roll.

That's the way I want it.
                    G5
Roll, roll, roll, gotta hear it loud,
                    D/F♯
Gonna take this town, turn it 'round.
                    G5
Gonna roll, roll, roll.

Outro

        C5   **D5**
I'm gonna   blow up my video,
C5   **D5**
   Shut down my radio.
                 F5
I told boss man where to go.
D5   **F5**
  Turned off my brain control.
A5
That's the way I want my rock 'n' roll.

That's the way I want my rock 'n' roll.

That's the way I wanna rock 'n' roll!

There's Gonna Be Some Rockin'

Words & Music by
Angus Young, Malcolm Young and Bon Scott

| *Intro* | ‖: **D** | | :‖ *play 4 times* |

D

Verse 1 Well, me and the boys,

Are out to have some fun.

Gonna put on a show,

Come on, let's go.

                   G

Chorus 1 There's gonna be some rockin'.
                   D
There's gonna be some rockin'.
                   A
There's gonna be some rockin'
G   **D**
  At the show tonight.

Verse 2 Every night,

There's a rock 'n' roll Queen.

Gonna quiver and quake,

Gonna shake her thing.

Chorus 2

      G
There's gonna be some rockin'.
      D
There's gonna be some rockin'.
      A
There's gonna be some rockin'
G   **D**
 At the show tonight.

Solo 1

D				
G		**D**		
A	**G**	**D**		

Verse 3

D
We got a big fat sound,

Wanna share it round.

Got a big bass drum,

Gonna have some fun.

Chorus 3

      G
There's gonna be some rockin'.
      D
There's gonna be some rockin'.
      A
There's gonna be some rockin'
G   **D**
 At the show tonight.

There's gonna be some rockin'.

There's gonna be some rockin'.
      G
There's gonna be some rockin'.

                                D
              There's gonna be some rockin'.
                                A
              There's gonna be some rockin'
              G   **D**
                At the show tonight.

Solo 2 | **D** | | | |
                | **G** | | **D** | |
                | **A** | **G** | **D** | |

Chorus 4   There's gonna be some rockin'.

               There's gonna be some rockin'.
                                G
               There's gonna be some rockin'
                                D
               There's gonna be some rockin'.
                                A
               There's gonna be some rockin'.
               G   **D**
                 At the show tonight.
                                A
               There's gonna be some rockin'.
               G   **D**
                 At the show tonight.
                                A
               There's gonna be some rockin'.
               G   **D5**
                 At the show tonight.

Thunderstruck

Words & Music by
Angus Young and Malcolm Young

Intro ‖: **B** | | | **Em** | | :‖
‖: **B** | | :‖

B
‖: Thunder ah, thunder, ah, :‖ *play 4 times*
B5
Thunder, thunder, thunder, thunder.

Verse 1 I was caught,

In the middle of a railroad track, (Thunder).

I looked round,

And I knew there was no turning back, (Thunder).

My mind raced,

And I thought, what could I do? (Thunder).

And I knew,

There was no help, no help from you, (Thunder).
         A5
Sound of the drums,
E5   **B5** **A5**
Beatin' in my heart,
   E5   **B5** **A5**
The thunder of guns,
E5   **B5** **A5** **E5**
Tore me apart.
B5
    You've been thunderstruck.

Verse 2   Rode down the highway,

Broke the limit, we hit the town.

Went through to Texas, yeah Texas,

And we had some fun.

We met some girls,

Some dancers who gave a good time.

Broke all the rules, played all the fools,
                                                              A5
Yeah, yeah, they, they, they blew our minds.
E5   **B5 A5**
  I was shakin' at the knees.
E5   **B5 A5**
  Could I come again please?
E5   **B5 A5**
  Yeah, the ladies were too kind.

   E5   **B5   A5 E5**
Chorus 1   You've been thunderstruck,
A5 E5   **B5   A5 E5**
     Thunderstruck,
A5   E5   **B5   A5 E5**
Yeah, yeah, yeah, thunderstruck,
A5 E5   **B5   A5 E5**
  Oh, thunderstruck, yeah.

Interlude | **A5 E5** |: **B5** | :|

  B5
I was shakin' at the knees,

Could I come again please?

Solo

```
‖: E5  B5  A5 |  E5   :‖  play 4 times
‖: B5  A5    |        :‖  play 4 times
 | B5        |
```

Chorus 2

                   B5   A5 E5
Thunderstruck,
A5 E5   **B5 A5 E5**
       Thunderstruck,
A5   **E5**   **B5 A5 E5**
Yeah, yeah, yeah, thunderstruck,
A5 E5   **B5**   **A5**   **E5**
     Thunderstruck, yeah, yeah, yeah.
          B5   **E5**
    Said, yeah, it's alright,
B5   **E5 B5**   **E5**
We're doing fine, yeah, it's alright,
B5   **E5**
We're doing fine, so fine.

Chorus 3

                  B5 A5 E5
Thunderstruck,
A5   **E5**   **B5**   **A5 E5**
Yeah, yeah, yeah, thunderstruck,
A5   **E5**   **B5**   **A5**
Thunderstruck, (Thunderstruck),
A5   **E5**   **B5**   **A5 E5**
Whoa baby, baby, thunderstruck,
A5   **E5**   **B5**   **A5 E5**
You've been thunderstruck,
 A5 E5   **B5**   **A5 E5**
‖:   Thunderstruck,
A5 E5   **B5**   **A5 E5**
     Thunderstruck,   :‖

You've been thunderstruck.
 | **B5**   ‖

Touch Too Much

Words & Music by
Angus Young, Malcolm Young and Bon Scott

Intro　　　　‖: **E5** 　　|　　 :‖

Verse 1

　　　　　　　E5
It was one of those nights,
　　　　　　　　C
When you turn out the lights,
　　A5　　　　　　　**Asus4 A Asus4 A**
And everything comes into view.
Asus4　　　　**E5**
　　　　　She was taking her time,
　　　C
I was losing my mind,
　　　　　　A5　　　　　　　**Asus4 A**
There was nothing that she wouldn't do.
Asus4 A A sus4　　**C**
　　　　　　　　It wasn't the first,

It wasn't the last.
　　　A5
She knew we was making love.
　　　C5
I was so satisfied,

Deep down inside,
　　　　D5
Like a hand in a velvet glove.

Chorus 1

　　　　　　　　E5　**G5**　　　　**A5**　**C5**
Seems like a touch,　　a touch too much.
D5　　　　**E5**　**G5**　　　　**A5**　**C5**
Seems like a touch,　　a touch too much.
D5　　**E5**　　　　　　　**G5**
　　Too much for my body, too much for my brain.
A5　　　　　　　　**C5**　　　**D5**
This damn woman's gonna drive me insane.
　　　　　　E5　**G5**　　　　**A5**
She's got a touch,　　a touch too much.

Link | D A5 D A5 D A5 | E5 | |

Verse 2

She had the face of an angel,
C
Smiling with sin,
  A5   **Asus4 A Asus4 A**
The body of Venus with arms.
Asus4 E5
      Dealing with danger,
C
Stroking my skin,
      A5   **Asus4 A Asus4**
Like a thunder and lightnin' storm.
A Asus4   C
         It wasn't the first,

It wasn't the last,
  A5
It wasn't that she didn't care.
   C5
She wanted it hard,

Wanted it fast,
  D5
She liked it done medium rare.

Chorus 2

            E5 G5   **A5 C5**
Seems like a touch,   a touch too much.
D5   **E5 G5**   **A5 C5**
Seems like a touch,   a touch too much.
D5   E5   **G5**
   Too much for my body, too much for my brain.
A5   **C5**   **D5**
This damn woman's gonna drive me insane.
          E5 G5   **E5**
She's got a touch,   a touch too much.

Touch me!

	C5		A5		

Solo

C5			A5		
C5			D5		
E5 G5 A5		B5	C5 A5 E5	

Bridge

                 E5   **G5**
Seems like a touch, touch too much.
                         A5   **D5**
You know it's much too much, much too much.
             E5   **G5**
I really want to feel yeah, touch too much.
                    A5   **D5**
Girl you know you're givin' me, much too much.
               E5 **G5**   **A5**
Oh, seems like a touch,   just a dirty little touch.
D5   **E5**
  I really need your touch,
G5   **A5**
   'Cause you're much too much too much too much.

Chorus 3

             E5 **G5**   **A5** **C5**
Seems like a touch,   a touch too much.
D   **E5** **G5**   **A5** **C5**
  Seems like a touch,   a touch too much.
D   **E5** **G5**   **A5** **C5**
  Givin' me a touch,   a touch too much.
D   **E5** **G5**   **A5** **C5**
  Baby got a touch,   a touch too much.
D   **E5**   **A5** **C5** **D E5**
Seems like a touch, a touch too much.

Outro

```
     G5          A5    C5 D E5
      A touch too much.
     G5          A5   C5 D E5
      A touch too much.
     G5          A5    D5 A5 D5 A5 D5 A5
      A touch too much.
          D5 A5 D5 A5
    Touch,
          D5 A5           D5 A5 D5 A5 D5 A5
    Come on,     touch me!
    E5
    Yeah!
```

Walk All Over You

Words & Music by
Angus Young, Malcolm Young and Bon Scott

Intro

‖: **E5** | **G5** **D5** | **A5** | :‖ *play 4 times*
‖: **E5** **G5** **D5** | **A** | :‖ *play 8 times*

Verse 1

E
Out of my way I'm running high.   **G5**
D   **E**   **G5**
  Take a chance with me and I'll give it a try.
D E   **G5**
  Ain't no woman in the world I know,
D   **A5**
  'Cause I ain't looking for a woman's love.

| **A5** **D5 A5** | **D5** **A5** |

Verse 2

E   **G5**
Oh baby I ain't got much,
D E   **G5**
  Resistance to your touch.
D E   **G5**
  Take off the high heels, let down your hair,
D A5
  Paradise ain't far from there.

Chorus 1

D5 A5   **D5**   **A5 E5**
  I wanna walk   all over you.
G5   **D5**   **E5**
  I wanna walk all over you.
G5   **D5**   **E5**
  Do anything you want me to, baby.
G5 D5   **A5**
  I wanna walk all over you.

| **A5** **D5 A5** | **D5** **A5** |

| *Link* | ‖: **E5 G5 D5** │ **A** ： ‖ *play 4 times* |

Verse 3

E   **G5**
Reflections on the bedroom wall,
D   E   **G5**
  And there you thought you'd seen it all.
D   E   **G5**
  We're rising, falling like the sea,
D   A5
  You're looking so good under me.

Chorus 2

D5 A5   D5 A5 E5
  I wanna walk   all over you.
G5   D5   E5
  I wanna walk all over you.
G5   D5   E5
  Do anything you want me to, baby.
G5 D5   A D/A A
  I wanna walk all over   you.
A D/A A D   A   D
     Now watch out!

Solo

‖: **E5   G5 D5** │ **A** ： ‖ *play 10 times*
│ **G5**   │ **A5**   │
│ **G5**   │ **A5**   │ **B5**   │
‖: **E5   G5 D5** │ **A** ： ‖ *play 4 times*

Verse 4

       E   **G5**
Around and round in the stereo,
D5   **E**   **G5**
   So gimme the stage, I'm gonna steal the show.
D5 E   **G5**
   Leave on the lace and turn off the light,
D5   **A5**
   Tonight is gonna be the night.

Chorus 3

D5 A5   **D5** **A5** **E5**
  I'm gonna walk   all over you.
G5   **D5**   **E5**
 I'm gonna walk all over you.
G5   **D5**   **E5**
  Do anything you want me to, baby.
G5   **D**   **E5**
  I'm gonna walk all over you, ow!

Who Made Who

Words & Music by
Angus Young and Malcolm Young and Brian Johnson

Intro

‖: **N.C.** | :‖
‖: **D5** | :‖

Verse 1

D5
The video games she play me.

Face it on a level, but it takes you,
B5
Every time on a one on one.
A5
Feel it running down your spine.

Nothing gonna save your one last dime,
D5
'Cause it owns you, through and through.

Verse 2

Dsus4
The databank knows my number.

Says I gotta pay,
B5
'Cause I made the grade last year.
A5
Feel it when I turn the screw.

Kicks you round the world,
D5
There ain't a thing that it can't do, do to you.

Chorus 1

D   **Dsus4**
Who made who?   Who made you?
D   **Dsus4**
Who made who? Ain't nobody told you.
D   **Dsus4**
Who made who?   Who made you?
      D   **Dsus4**
If you made them and they made you,
                      A A7sus4
Who pick up the middle, and who made who?
D/A A   **A7sus4 D/A**
      Yeah!
A   **D**   **Dsus 4**   **D Dsus4**
   Who made who?   Who turned the screw?

Solo

‖: **B5** | :‖
| **A A7sus4 D/A** | **A** | **Gm** | |

Verse 3

D   **Dsus4**
Satellites send me pictures.
D   **Dsus4**
Get it in the eye, take it to the wire,
               B5
Spinning like a dynamo.
A7sus4
Feel it goin' round and round.

Running out of chips,
               D   **Dsus4**
You got no line in a naked town.
      D   **Dsus4**
So don't look down,   no!

	D	**Dsus4**
Chorus 2	Who made who?	Who made you?
	D	**Dsus4**
	Who made who? Ain't nobody told you.	
	D	**Dsus4**
	Who made who?	Who made you?
	D	**Dsus4**
	If you made them and they made you,	
		A A7sus4
	Who pick up the middle, and who made who?	
	D/A A	**A7sus4 D/A**
	Yeah!	
	A	**D** **Dsus 4** **D Dsus4**
	Who made who?	Who turned the screw?

Outro

: **A**		**G D A**	
A G D	**A**	**G D**	
: **A**		:	*repeat to fade*

Whole Lotta Rosie

Words & Music by
Ronald Scott, Angus Young and Malcolm Young

Intro

```
|: A5   D5   A5 |          :| play 4 times
|  A5   D5   A5 |
```

Verse 1

N.C.
Wanna tell you a story,
| A5   D5   A5 |

N.C.
'Bout a woman I know.
| A5   D5   A5 |

N.C.
Ah, when come to lovin',
| A5   D5   A5 |

N.C.
She steals the show.
| A5   D5   A5 |

N.C.
She ain't exactly pretty,
| A5   D5   A5 |

N.C.
Ain't exactly small.
| A5   D5   A5 |

N.C.
Forty-two, thirty-nine, fifty-six

You could say she's got it all.

Interlude

```
|: A5   D5   A5 :| play 9 times
```

Verse 2

A5
Never had a woman,
        D5   A5
Never had a woman like you.
D5 A5
   Doing all the things,
        D5   A5
Doing all the things you do.
D5 A5   D5
  Ain't no fairy story,
A5
  Ain't no skin and bones.
D5   A5
   But you give it all you got,
        D5   A5
Weighing in at nineteen stone.

Chorus 1

                 F5   D5
You're a whole lotta woman, a whole lotta woman.
         A5   G5   A5   G5
Whole lotta Rosie,   whole lotta Rosie,
         A5
Whole lotta Rosie,
               G5   D5 G5
And you're a whole lotta woman.

| D5 G5 G♯5 ‖: A5 D5 A5 :‖

A5

Verse 3 Oh honey you can do it,
                    D5   **A5**
Do it to me all night long.
D5 A5
    Only one to turn,
                    D5   **A5**
Only one to turn me on.
D5 A5   **D5**
    All through the night time,
A5
    And right around the clock.
D5   **A5**
    To my surprise,
          D5   **A5**
Rosie never stops.

                                    F5   **D5**
Chorus 2   You're a whole lotta woman, a whole lotta woman.
                          A5   **G5**   **A5**   **G5**
Whole lotta Rosie,   whole lotta Rosie,
                          A5
Whole lotta Rosie,
                                    G5   **D5** **G5**
And you're a whole lotta woman.

| **D5**   **G5**   **G♯5** |

Solo   ‖: **A5**   **D5**   **A5** | :‖ *play 7 times*
         | **A5** | | **F5** | |
         | **D5** | |
         ‖: **A5** | **D5 A5** :‖ *play 6 times*
         | **(A)** | | **A5** | **D5 A5** |
         ‖: **A5** | **D5 A5** :‖ *play 7 times*
         | **A5** | |

	F5 D5
Chorus 3	You're a whole lotta woman, a whole lotta woman.

                               A5   G5   **A5   G5**

Whole lotta Rosie,   whole lotta Rosie,

                                A5

Whole lotta Rosie,

                              G5   D5 G5

And you're a whole lotta woman.

| D5 G5 G♯5 |

Outro	‖: **A5**	**D5 A5** :‖ *play 12 times*
	A5	:‖ *play 6 times*
	‖: **G5**	
	A5	:‖
	A5	

You Shook Me All Night Long

Words & Music by
Angus Young, Malcolm Young and Brian Johnson

Intro

```
‖: G      |        | D      |         :‖
‖: G   C | G  C  G  D |   G | D  G  D :‖
```

Verse 1

```
        D    G              C        G
She was a fast machine, she kept her motor   clean.
C    G   D                    G      D
   She was the best damn woman that I've ever seen.
G    D     G            C          G C
   She had the sightless eyes, telling me no   lies,
G D                              G      D  G
   Knockin' me out with those American thighs.
D      G               C           G C
Taking more than her share, had me fighting for air.
G    D                    G      D G
   She told me to come but I was already there.
D      G                C         G  C
'Cause the walls start shakin', the earth was quakin',
G   D             Dsus4     D Dsus4 D
My mind was aching, and we were   making  it.
```

Chorus 1

```
      G           Cadd9 G/B  D    Cadd9
And you, shook me all      night long.
G/B    G              Cadd9 G/B D
   Yeah, you shook me all      night long.
```

Verse 2

G/B   G   C   G
     Working double time, on the seduction   line.
C G D   G   D
     She was one of a kind, she's just mine all mine.
G D   G   C   G   C
     Wanted no applause, just another course.
G   D   G   D G
Made a meal out of me and came back for more.
D   G   C   G   C
Had to cool me down, to take another round.
G   D   G   D   G
Now I'm back in the ring to take another swing.
D   G   C   G C
'Cause the walls start shakin', the earth was quakin',
G D   Dsus4   D Dsus4 D
My mind was aching, and we were making it.

Chorus 2

G/B G   Cadd9 G/B D   Cadd9
‖ And you, shook me all   night long.
G/B   G   Cadd9 G/B D
     Yeah, you shook me all   night long. ‖

```
| G        C |  G/B    D|           C |  G/B    G |
|        Cadd9 |         D|       Cadd9 |  G/B      |
| G      Cadd9 |  G/B    D|       Cadd9 |  G/B      |
| G      Cadd9 |  G/B    D|             |
```

G/B G   **Cadd9 G/B D   Cadd9**

Chorus 3   ‖: And you, shook me all   night long.

G/B   G   **Cadd9 G/B D**

      Yeah, you shook me all   night long. :‖

         G/B   D

Yeah, you shook me

Cadd9   **G/B   D**

      Yeah, you shook me,

All night long.

Chord Finder

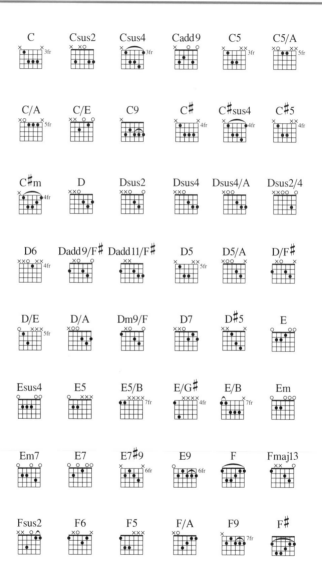

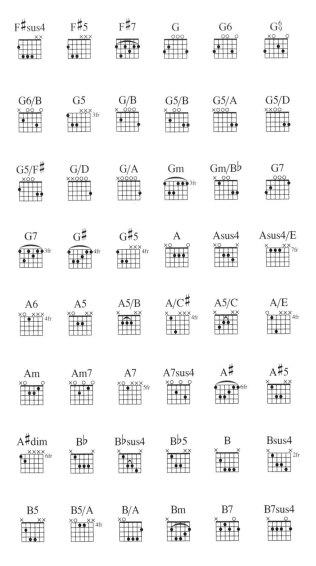